Christian Leadership
By Choice and by Appointment
Revised Edition

Benjamin A. Van Winkle

Ocala, FL

Copyright © 2010, 2017 Benjamin A. Van Winkle

All rights reserved. No part of this publication may be reproduced, distributed, or transmitted in any form or by any means, including photocopying, recording, or other electronic or mechanical methods, without the prior written permission of the publisher, except in the case of brief quotations embodied in critical reviews and certain other noncommercial uses permitted by copyright law. For permission requests, write to the publisher, addressed "Attention: Permissions Coordinator," at the address below.

Zeta Publishing, Inc
3850 SE 58th Ave
Ocala, FL 34480
www.zetapublishing.com

The views expressed in this work are solely those of the author and do not necessarily reflect the views of the publisher, and the publisher hereby disclaims any responsibility for them.

Ordering Information:
Quantity sales. Special discounts are available on quantity purchases by corporations, associations, and others. For details, contact the publisher at the address above.
Orders by U.S. trade bookstores and wholesalers. Please contact Zeta Publishing: Tel: (352) 694-2553; Fax: (352) 694-1791 or visit www.zetapublishing.com

First published by Xlibris in 8/12/2010

Rev. Date: Sept 2017

ISBN: 978-1-947191-45-7 (sc)
ISBN: 978-1-947191-46-4 (e)

Library of Congress: 2017956381
Printed in the United States of America

Contents

Leadership in the Old Testament 1
Charismatic Leaders 4
Religious Leaders 6
Leadership in the Old Testament 7
Charismatic Leaders of the Old Testament 21
Religious Leaders of the Old Testament 25
We Come Now to the New Testament 27
Religious Leaders 28
Charismatic Leaders 30
Theological Dimensions of Leadership 30
Leaders in Our Day 31
Functions of Management 34
Principles of Management 34
Some Key Terms of Management 36
Leadership and Management Compared 39
Performance 41
Limitations 41
Chain of Command 42
Motivational Factors 45
Leadership Theory 46
The Democratic Concept; Government Leaders 51
An Approach to Basic Leadership Training 52
Interviews 53
The Leaders 54
Attitudes, Styles, and Personality 56
Important: Suggestions Would Be as Follows 58
Promotions 60
Timing; Assistance; Cost 60
Planning and Organization 61
Transfer of Work/Authority, Acceptance of
Responsibility, and the Importance of Follow-up 62
Work to Be Delegated 62
Rules of Delegation 63
There Is Also Controlling 63
Another Ingredient Is Time Management 64

Guidance..64
New Testament Scripture References from NKJV...................................66
Charismatic Leaders..70
Theological Dimensions of Leadership..71
Leaders are Accountable..80
Faith and Leadership..81

Christian Leadership
By Choice and by Appointment

This material has been put together from a personal viewpoint; hopefully it, will inspire some of the people who read it to step out into the ranks of leadership with renewed hope and ambitions.

Leadership in the Old Testament

In the earliest days of old, leadership of the people of God was by the family head or patriarch, to whom God spoke His messages.

Civil Leaders: By the time of Exodus, tribal elders were on the scene. We're not told how they were appointed. They served as representatives for the whole nation (Exod. 3:16, 4:29, 12:21), but without any apparent initiative or governing power. On occasion Moses was told by God to assemble them to impart to them and through them to the people, God's Message (Exod. 3:16, 4:29, 12:21, 19:7; Josh. 24:1). They accompanied Moses and Joshua following the sins of Dathan and Abiram (Num. 16:25) and Achan (Josh. 7:6). Moses selected seventy of them to be specially endued with God's Spirit to help share the burden of the people (Num. 11:16-17). By the time of the judges and the monarchy were elders of Israel who made common decisions such as the appointment of a king. There were elders in the individual towns (Judg. 11:3-11; 1 Sam. 16:4, 30:26-31; 1 Kings 21:8, 11).

1 Samuel 30:26-31 indicates that the elders of Judah were comprised of the elders of the individual towns, though later Ezekiel speaks of "seventy elders of Israel" These seventy represented the nation's leaders (Num. 11). Here each man carried a vessel for burning incense. Each man here seems to have his own god. The emphasis here is on each elder's pagan beliefs and their secret behavior in the dark. Ironically, they thought of God in limited human terms, much like how their neighbors viewed their own gods. They thought He was not omniscient and omnipresent (Ezek. 8:11-12). The local elders were responsible for legal action at the city gate (Deut. 22:15, 25:7; Ruth 4:1-11), in cases of murder (Deut. 19:11-13, 21:1-9) and in cases dealing with family matters (Deut. 21:18-21, 22:13-21, 25:5-10).

During the exile, there were elders in Judah (Ezek. 8:11-12). They opposed Jehoiakim and pleaded with the people on behalf of Jeremiah (Jer. 26:17). In exile there were elders heading the community (Jer. 29: l; Ezek. 8:1, 14:1, 20:1, 3). The elders stood at the head of the people in the rebuilding of the temple and even dealing with the Persian government (Ezra 5:9, 6:7, 8, 14). The system of city elders is evident when Ezra resolved to excommunicate those who had married foreign wives (Ezra 10:8, 14). By Nehemiah's time, the elders are referred to as the nobility (Neh. 2:16, 4:14, 19, 5:7, 7:5).

The call for a king came from the people toward the end of Samuel's judgeship. The people were no longer satisfied to have God as their king, and God viewed their request as a rejection of Himself (1 Sam. 8:7, 12:12). In the end, God told Samuel to listen to the people. He anointed Saul and told him that he was anointed by the Lord (1 Sam. 10:1, 12:13).

There were three subsequent errors on Saul's part (chapters 13, 14, 15).

He showed that his heart had become proud (l Sam. 15:17), and he no longer fully obeyed the Lord. The Lord regretted having made him king, and Saul's kingdom was not established forever as it might have been (1 Sam. 13:13).

In Saul's place, God had Samuel anoint David, a man whose perspective was in line with God's (13:14). With him God made a covenant forever that forecast that any well being would be by his appointment, and that any necessary correction he would accomplish through their enemies (2 Sam. 7:9-16). Care had been taken already in Deuteronomy to warn future kings against self-indulgence, against lifting themselves up above their fellow countrymen. Pride spelled ruin. On the positive side, faith, along with obedience was a determiner of success (Deut.17:14-20).

These were the terms of the theocracy. David's son Solomon began to rule following in his father's footsteps; but in the course of his reign, he multiplied for himself horses, wives, silver and gold, all three areas against which Deuteronomy had sounded a warning. His foreign wives turned him away from trusting in God, and for this the Lord said He would tear from him the kingdom and give it to his servants, leaving him but one tribe for his father's sake (1 Kings 11:1-13, chapter 12).

We are especially careful to point out how the successors in David's line failed to meet the terms of the theocracy. For example, through a prophet, Asa was told that if he sought the Lord, he would let him find Him; but if he forsook God, God would forsake him (2 Chron. 15:2). Hezekiah sought the Lord with all his heart and prospered (31:21) until he became proud (32:25). Subsequent humbling postponed God's wrath during Hezekiah's time (32:26), as it did again near the end of Manasseh's wicked reign (33:9-19). In summary, God warned the kings again and again for their unfaithfulness, sending them His messengers, the prophets, but they did not listen until finally God moved in wrath to judge them at the hands of the Babylonians (36:12-16). When the ten northern tribes seceded from Judah, the Davidic covenant did not apply to their kings, but the issue of obedience as outlined in Deuteronomy still applied. Jeroboam, their first king, set up the calf cult at Dan and Bethel. For this, his own family line was blotted off the face of the earth (1 Kings 13:33-34), and for this eventually the whole kingdom went into captivity (2 Kings 17:16-18). The king who followed Jeroboam persisted in his ungodly direction.

After Jerusalem fell to the Babylonians, Judah was ruled by governors chosen by Babylon and Persia, some at least from Judean royal blood (2 Kings 25:22, Gedaliah; Zerubbabel, 1 Chron. 3:10-19). Not that this was different from the situation just prior to Jerusalem's fall, the king then, too, withered and were set up and removed at the will of foreign powers. Jehoiakim favored over his brother by Egypt and Zedekiah over his nephew by Babylon (2 Chron. 36:3, 10); Nehemiah's lineage is not recorded. He was recognized by the Persian king for his faithfulness in service as his cupbearer and for his concern for his own people back in Jerusalem. Faith and obedience were still integral to God's blessings on leadership.

Charismatic Leaders

The Old Testament leader par excellence was Moses. Unlike others, God spoke directly to him (Num. 12:6-8). At the age of forty, he expected that his people would recognize him as God's appointed leader to bring their deliverance, but this first initiative was prematurely aborted, and he fled the country (Acts 7:23-29). Forty years later, he was clearly called of God, and this time he returned to Egypt and first gained the support of the elders of Israel (Exod. 4:29-31). Through signs and wonders, his people and also the people of Egypt came to recognize him as God's man. At Sinai, the law and the tabernacle instructions were given to Moses to pass along to the people. He acted on behalf of God at the installation of Aaron and his sons to the priesthood. On occasion, God needed to vindicate Moses's leadership before the people (Exod. 16; Num. 12-13). God viewed their mumbling against Moses as against Him (Exod. 16:7-8). Conversely, Moses was held accountable when he broke faith and did not represent God as holy in the sight of the people (Num. 20:12). For this, he was disallowed entrance into the promise land.

He did actively prepare a successor, Joshua, and the people to accept him as their leader under God (Deut. 31:2-8).

Joshua began his period of leadership with a challenge from God to take courage. If he obeyed carefully, God would have granted him success in taking over the land of the Canaanites (Josh. 1:2-9). The Lord appoints Joshua as leader. Joshua must arise to the task and finish the work Moses began.

Having accomplished chat goal by the end of his life, he apparently did-not see a need to prepare a successor.

The judges were charismatic leaders raised up by God (Judg. 2:16) to deliver His people. Their work was both military and supervisory in kind, and though not all were involved in the military, this is the aspect chat comprises much of the biblical record, and therefore, for which they are best known. Likely their activities normally resulted from their military success (Deborah is an exception). The judges seem to have been involved in supervisory activity; no military involvement is mentioned for four of them. Their area of jurisdiction was local, sometimes extending to several tribes, and their judgeship apparently overlapped (Jephthah and Samson;

Judg. 10:7). Though the law did not prescribe the office of judge, it was approved by God, for scripture states that He raised up judges (Judg. 3:9, 15), and at least four were especially enabled by the Holy Spirit (3:10, 6:34, 11:29, 13:25, 14:6, 19, 15:14). None of them appointed successors to carry on their work. In the two instances where sons attempted to carry on in their father's footsteps, they did not succeed (Gideon's son; Abimelech and Samuel's sons).

Jeremiah 18:18 speaks of the priests, the prophets, and the counselors. At David's court, there were permanent counselors (1 Chron. 27:32-33). These were men recognized and chosen for their wisdom. It was said of Ahithophel that his advice was as if one inquired of the word of God.

The prophets/prophetesses were God's mouth to the people similarly as Aaron was Moses's mouth (Exod. 4:16). They spoke out to kings, princes, priests, false prophets, people, and even nations. Elisha rook God's message to Syria (2 Kings 8), Jonah to Nineveh, and Ezekiel preached among the exiles in Babylon.

But most of their attention was focused on Israel. God sent prophets to sound a warning, before the northern kingdom fell to Assyria (Amos, Hosea, Isaiah, Micah) and before Babylon took Judah (Zephaniah, Habakkuk, Jeremiah, Ezekiel). Since they recorded their messages, future generations had to take notice that they had been warned.

How the prophets were received was in direct proportion to God's intervention to their audience, the rulers in particular. Samuel's influence with the people was strong enough that Saul didn't think of harming him. David bowed to Nathan's condemnation, Isaiah and Hezekiah worked well together, Jeremiah mourned Josiah's death, and Haggi and Zechariah collaborated with Zerubbabel to get the temple rebuilt. But others fared worse, for example, Elijah with Ahab and Jezebel, Amos with Jeroboam and Amaziah, priests of the Bethel calf cult, and Jeremiah with Josiah's three reigning sons and grandson. It's difficult to be a leader if the people are unwilling to follow.

Religious Leaders

The official leaders in Israel were the priests, headed by the high priest. Their office was hereditary, with the eldest living son of the high priest continuing his father's position, while God charged all Israel to be a people that functioned in a priestly ministry to the world (Exod. 19:6). It was Aaron and his family who were consecrated to do the service of the tabernacle (Lev. 8).

Their ordination ceremony was repeated on seven successive days-surely an indication to all that they were especially set apart for their priestly ministry.

The priests had several functions:

1. Primarily, they were to mediate between God and man. In following the ordinances of God, they led the people in acquiring atonement for their sins.
2. They were to represent the holiness of God to the people. Their garments were "for glory and beauty." The high priest especially, and on his plate was of pure gold like the engraving of a signet "Holiness to Yahweh" (Exod. 28:2, 36). When the high priest represented the people to God on the day of atonement, he wore plain white garments. Physical wholeness and exemplary conduct and character were requisites for the priesthood (Lev. 21, 22:9).
3. The priests were to render the will of God by means of the Urim and Thummin worn by the high priest on the breastplate (Num. 27:21).
4. It was their responsibility to instruct the laity in the distinction between holy and profane, clean and unclean (Lev. 10:10-11).

From the day of the first Passover in Egypt the firstborn of every household especially belonged to God. After the golden calf incident, it was the tribe of Levi who stood out to count themselves on the Lord's side (Exod. 32:26), and therefore they took the place of the firstborn (Num. 8:14-19). At their induction, they were sprinkled and offered as a wave offering a kind of living sacrifice. Their function was twofold.

1. They were to assist their brothers, the priests, in the service of the tabernacle from age thirty to fifty (Num. 4:3).
2. They were to keep watch over the tabernacle, to do guard duty from the age of one-month old and upward by living around the tabernacle. Their

dwelling formed the buffer zone to prevent others from incurring God's wrath by approaching too near to this Holy spot (Num.1:53, 3:28, 8:19).

Leadership in the Old Testament
Old Testament Scripture References from New King James Bible

Exodus 3:16:	Go and gather the elders of Israel together, and say to them, "The Lord God of your fathers, the God of Abraham, of Isaac, and of Jacob, appeared to me, saying, 'I have surely visited you and seen what is done to you in Egypt;
Exodus 4:29:	Then Moses and Aaron went and gathered together all the elders of the children of Israel.
Exodus 12:21:	Then Moses called for all the elders of Israel and said to them, "Pick out and take lambs for yourselves according to your families, and kill the Passover lamb.
Exodus 19:7:	So Moses came and called for the elders of the people, and laid before them all these words which the Lord commanded him.
Joshua 24:1:	Then Joshua gathered all the tribes of Israel to Shechem and called for the elders of Israel, for their heads, and for their judges, and for their officers, and they presented themselves before God.
Numbers 16:25:	Then Moses rose and went to Dathan and Abiram, and the elders of Israel followed him.
Joshua 7:6:	Then Joshua tore his clothes, and fell to the earth on his face before the ark of the Lord until evening, he and the elders of Israel, and they put dust on their heads.
Numbers 11:16, 17:	So the Lord said to Moses, "Gather to me seventy men of the elders of Israel, whom you know to be

the elders of the people and officers over them; bring them to the tabernacle of meeting, that they may stand with you.

V. 17: Then I will come down and talk with you there. I will take of the Spirit that is upon you and will put the same upon them; and they shall bear the burden of the people with you, that you may not bear it yourself alone.

Judges 11:3-11
V. 3: Then Jephthah fled from his brothers and dwelt in the land of Tod; and worthless men banded together with Jephthah and went out raiding with him.
V. 4: It came to pass after a time that the people of Ammon made war against Israel.
V. 5: And so it was, when the people of Ammon made war against Israel, that the elder of Gilead went to get Jephthah from the land of Tod.
V. 6: Then they said to Jephthah, "Come and be our commander, that we may fight against the people of Ammon."
V. 7: So Jephthah said to the elder of Gilead, "Did you not hate me, and expel me from my father's house? Why have you come to me now when you are in distress?"
V. 8: And the elder of Gilead said to Jephthah, "That is why we have turned again to you now, that you may go with us and fight against the people of Ammon, and be our head over all the inhabitants of Gilead."
V. 9: So Jephthah said to the elder of Gilead, "If you take me back home to fight against the people of Ammon, and the Lord delivers them to me shall I be your head?"
V. 10: And the elder of Gilead said to Jephthah, "The Lord will be a witness between us, if we do not do according to your words."
V. 11: Then Jephthah went with the people of Gilead, and the people made him head and commander over them; and Jephthah spoke all his words before the Lord in Mizpah.

1 Samuel 16:4: So Samuel did what the Lord said and went to Bethlehem. And the elders of the town trembled at his coming, and said, "Do you come peaceably?

1 Samuel 30:26-31
V. 26: Now when David came to Zikleg, he sent some of the spoil to the elders of Judah, to his friends saying, "Here is a present for you from the spoil of the enemies of the Lord"
V. 27: to those who were in Bethel, those who were in Ramoth of the South, those who were in Jattir,
V. 28: those who were in Aroer, those who were in Siphmoth, those who were in Eshtemoa,
V. 29: those who were in Rachal, those who were in the city of the Jerahmeelites, those who were in the city of the Kenites,
V. 30: those who were in Hormah, those who were in Chorashan, those who were in Athach,
V. 31: those who were in Hebron, and to all the place where David himself and his men were accustomed to rove.

1 Kings 21: 8, 11
V. 8: And she wrote letters in Ahab's name, sealed them with his seal, and sent the letters to the elders and nobles who were dwelling in the city with Naboth.
V. 11: So the men of his city, the elders and nobles who were inhabitants of his city, did as Jezebel had sent to them, as it was written in the letters which she had sent to them.

Ezekiel 8:11-12
V. 11: and there stood before them seventy men of the elders of the house of Israel, and in their midst stood Jaazaniah the son of Shaphan. Each man had a censer in his hand, and a thick cloud of incense went up.
V. 12: then he said to me, "Son of man, have you seen what the elders of the house of Israel do in the dark, every man in the room of his idols? For they say, 'The Lord does not see us, the Lord has forsaken the land.'"

Deuteronomy 22:15: Then the father and mother of the young woman shall take and bring out the evidence of the young woman's virginity to the elders of the city at the gate.

Deuteronomy 25:7: But if the man does not want to take his brother's wife, then let his brother's wife go up to the gate to the elders, and say, "My husband's brother refuses to raise up a name to his brother in Israel, he will not perform the duty of my husband's brother."

Ruth 4:1-11

V. 1: Now Boaz went up to the gate and sat down there; and behold, the dose relative of whom Boaz spoke came by. So Boaz said, "Come aside, friend sit down here." So he came aside and sat down.

V. 2: And he took ten men of the elders of the city, and said, "Sit down here." So they sat down.

V. 3: Then he said to the dose relative, Naomi, who has come back from the country of Moab, sold the piece of land which belonged to our brother Elimelech.

V. 4: And I thought to inform you, saying, "Buy it back in the presence of the inhabitants the elders of my people. If you will redeem it, redeem it, but if you will not redeem it, then tell me, that I may know; for there is no one but you to redeem it, and I am next after you." And he said, "I will redeem it."

V. 5: Then Boaz said, "On the day you buy the field from the hand of Naomi, you must also buy it from Ruth the Moabitess, the wife of the dead, to perpetuate the name of the dead through his inheritance."

V. 6: And the dose relative said, "I cannot redeem it for myself, lest I ruin my own inheritance. You redeem my right of redemption for yourself, for I cannot redeem it."

V. 7: Now this was the custom in former times in Israel concerning redeeming and exchanging, to confirm anything: one man took off his sandal and gave it to the other, and this was a confirmation in Israel.

V. 8: Therefore the close relative said to Boaz, "Buy it for yourself" So he took off his sandal.

V. 9: And Boaz said to the elders and all the people, "You are witnesses today that I have bought all that was Elimelech's, and that was Chilion's and Mahlon's, from the hand of Naomi.

V. 10: Moreover, Ruth the Moabitess, the widow of Mahlon, I have acquired as my wife, to perpetuate the name of the dead through his inheritance, that the name of the dead may not be cut off from among his brethren and from his position at the gate. You are witnesses chis day."

V. 11: And all the people who were at the gate, and the elders said, "We are witnesses. The Lord make the woman who is coming to your house like Rachel and Leah, the two who built the house of Israel; and may you prosper in Ephrathah and be famous in Bethlehem.

Deuteronomy 19:11-13
V. 11: But if any one hates his neighbor, or lies in wait for him, rises against him and strikes him mortally, so that he dies, and he flees to one of these cities,
V. 12: then the elders from his city shall send and bring him from there, and deliver him over to the hand of the avenger of blood, chat he may die.
V. 13: Your eye shall not pity him, but you shall put away the guile of innocent blood from Israel, that it may go well with you.

Deuteronomy 21:1-9
V. 1: If anyone is found slain, lying in the field in the land which the Lord your God is giving you to possess, and it is not known who killed him,
V. 2: then your elders and your judges shall go out and measure the distance from the slain man to the surrounding cities.
V. 3: and it shall be that the elders of the city nearest the slain man will take a heifer which has not been worked, and which has not pulled with a yoke.
V. 4: The elders of that city shall bring the heifer down to a valley with flowing water, which is neither plowed nor sown, and they shall break the heifer's neck there in the valley.
V. 5: then the priests, the sons of Levi, shall come near, for the Lord you God has chosen them to minister to Him and to bless in the name of the Lord; by their word every controversy and every assault shall be settled.
V. 6: And all the elders of that city nearest the slain man, shall wash their hands over the heifer whose neck was broken in the valley.
V. 7: Then they shall answer and say, "Our hands have not shed this blood, nor have our eyes seen it.
V. 8: Provide atonement, 0 Lord, for your people Israel, whom you have redeemed, and do not lay innocent blood to the charge of your people Israel. And atonement shall be provided on their behalf for the blood.
V. 9: So you shall put away the guilt of innocent blood from among you when you do what is right in the sight of the Lord.

Deuteronomy 21:18-21

V. 18: If a man has a stubborn and rebellious son who will not obey the voice of his father or the voice of his mother, and who when they have chastened him, will not heed them,

V. 19: then his father and mother shall take hold of him and bring him out to the elders of the city, to the gate of his city.

V. 20: and they shall say to the elders of the city, "This son of ours is stubborn and rebellious; he will not obey our voice; he is a glutton and a drunkard."

V. 21: Then all the men of his city shall stone him to death with stones; so shall put away the evil from among you, and all Israel shall hear and fear.

Deuteronomy 22:13-21

V. 13: If any man takes a wife and goes in to her and detests her

V. 14: and charges her with shameful conduct, and brings a bad name on her, and says, "I took this woman, and when I came to her I found she was not a virgin,"

V. 15: then the father and mother of the young woman shall take and bring out the evidence of the young woman's virginity to the elders of the city at the gate.

V. 16: and the young woman's father shall say to the elders, "I gave my daughter to this man as wife, and he detests her."

V. 17: Now he has charged her with shameful conduct, saying, "I found your daughter was not a virgin," and yet these are the evidences of my daughter's virginity, and they shall spread the doth before the elders of the city.

V. 18: Then the elders of that city shall take that man and punish him.

V. 19: and they shall fine him one hundred shekels of silver and give them to the father of the young woman, because he has brought a bad name on a virgin of Israel. And she shall be his wife; he cannot divorce her all his days.

V. 20: But if the thing is true, and evidences of virginity are not found for the young woman,

V. 21: then they shall bring out the young woman to the door of her father's house, and the men of her city shall stone her to death with stones, because she has done a disgraceful thing in Israel, to play the harlot in her father's house. So you shall put away the evil from among you.

Deuteronomy 25:5-10

V. 5: If brothers dwell together, and one of them dies and has no son, the widow of the dead man shall not be married to a stranger outside the family; her husband's brother shall go in to her, take her as his wife, and perform the duty of a husband's brother.

V. 6: and it shall be that the firstborn son which she bears will succeed to the name of his dead brother, that his name may not be blotted out of Israel.

V. 7: But if the man does not want to take his brother's wife, then let his brother's wife go up to the gate to the elders and say, "My husband's brother refuses to raise up a name to his brother in Israel; he will not perform the duty of my husband's brother."

V. 8: Then the elders of the city shall call him and speak to him. But if he stands firm and says, "I do not want to take her,"

V. 9: then his brother's wife shall come to him in the presence of the elders, remove his sandal from his foot, spit in his face, and answer and say, 'So shall it be done unto the man who will not build up his brother's house.'

V. 10: And his name shall be called in Israel, 'The house of him who had his sandal removed.'

Jeremiah 26:17: Then certain of the elders of the land rose up and spoke to all the assembly of the people, saying

Jeremiah 29:1: Now these are the words of the letter that Jeremiah the profit sent from Jerusalem to the remainder of the elders who were carried away captive-to the priests, the prophets, and all the people whom Nebuchadnezzar had carried away captive from Jerusalem to Babylon.

Ezekiel 8: 1: and it came to pass in the sixth year, in the sixth month, on the fifth day of the month, as I sat in my house with the elders of Judah sitting before me, that the hand of the Lord God fail upon me there.

Ezekiel 14:1: Now some of the elders of Israel came to me and sat before me.

Ezekiel 20:1, 3

V. 1: It came to pass in the seventh year, in the fifth month, on the tenth day of the month, that certain of the elders of Israel came to inquire of the Lord, and sat before me.

V. 3: Son of man, speak to the elders of Israel, and say to them, "Thus says the Lord your God: Have you come to inquire of me? As I live," says the Lord God, "I will not be inquired of by you."

Ezra 5:9: Then we ask those elders, and spoke thus to them: We commanded you to build the temple and to finish these walls?

Ezra 6:7, 8, 14
V. 7: Let the work of this house of God alone; let the governor of the Jews and the elders of the Jews build this house of God on its site.
V. 8: Moreover I issue a decree as to what you shall do for the elders of these Jews, for the building of this house of God: Let the cost be paid at the king's expense from taxes on the region beyond the river; this is to be given immediately to these men, so that they are not hindered.
V. 14: So the elders of the Jews built, and they prospered through the prophesying of Haggai the profit and Zechariah the son of Iddo. And they built and finished it, according to the commandments of the God of Israel, and according to the command of Cyrus, Darius, and Artaxerxes king of Persia.

Ezra 10:8, 14
V. 8: and that whoever would not come within three days, according to the instruction of the leaders and elders, all his property would be confiscated, and he himself would be separated from the assembly of those from the captivity.
V. 14: Please, let leaders of our entire assembly stand; and let all those in our cities who have taken pagan wives come at appointed times, together with the elders and judges of their cities, until the fierce wrath of God is turned away from us in this matter.

Nehemiah 2:16: And the officials did not know where I had gone or what I had done; I had not yet told the Jews, the priests, the nobles, the officials, or the others who did the work.

Nehemiah 4: 14, 19: And I looked, and arose and said to the nobles, to the leaders, and to the rest of the people, "Do not be afraid of them. Remember the Lord, great and awesome, and fight for your brethren, your sons, your daughters, your wives, and your houses."

V. 19: Then I said to the nobles, the rulers, but the rest of the people, "The work is great and extensive, and we are separated far from one another on the wall.

Nehemiah 5:7: After serious thought, I rebuked the nobles and rulers, and said to them, "Each of you is exacting usury from his brother." So I called a great assembly against them.

Nehemiah 7:5: Then my God put it into my heart to gather the nobles, the rulers, and the people, that they might be registered by genealogy. And I found a register of genealogy of those who had come up in the first return, and found written in it.

1 Samuel 8:7: And the Lord said to Samuel, "Heed the voice of the people in all that they say to you; for they have not rejected you, but they have rejected me, that I should not reign over them.

1 Samuel 12:12: And when you saw that Nahash king of the Ammonites came against you, you said to me, "No, but a king shall reign over us," when the Lord your God was your king.

1 Samuel 10:1: Then Samuel took a flask of oil and poured it on his head, and kissed him and said: "Is it not because the Lord has anointed you commander over His inheritance?

1 Samuel 12:13: Now therefore, here is the king whom you have chosen and whom you have desired. And take note, the Lord has set a king over you.

1 Samuel 13

V. 1: Saul reigned one year; and when he had reigned two years over Israel,

V. 2: 14; 15

1 Samuel 15:17: So Samuel said, "When you were little in your own eyes, were you not head of the tribe of Israel? And did not the Lord anoint you king over Israel?

1 Samuel 13:13: And Samuel said to Saul, "You have done foolishly. You have not kept the commandments of the Lord your God, which He commanded you. For now the Lord would have established your kingdom over Israel forever.

1 Samuel 13:14: But now your kingdom will not continue. The lord has sought for Himself a man after His own heart, and the Lord has commanded him to be commander over His people, because you have not kept what the Lord has commanded you.

2 Samuel 7:9-16

V. 9: And I have been with you wherever you have gone, and have cut off your enemies from before you, and have made you a great name, like the name of the great men who are on the earth.

V. 10: Moreover I will appoint a place for my people Israel, and will plant them, that they might dwell in a place of their own and move no more, nor shall the sons of wickedness oppress them anymore, as previously

V. 11: since the time that I commanded judges to be over my people Israel, and have caused you to rest from all your enemies. Also the Lord tells you He will make you a house.

V. 12: When your days are fulfilled and you rest with your fathers, I will set up your seed after you, who will come from your body, and I will establish his kingdom.

V. 13: He shall build a house for my name, and I will establish the throne of his kingdom forever.

V. 14: I will be his father, and he shall be my son. If he commits iniquity, I will chasten him with the rod of men and with the blows of the sons of men.

V. 15: But my mercy shall not depart from him, as I took it from Saul, whom I removed from before you.

V. 16: And your house and your kingdom shall be established forever before you. Your throne shall be established forever.

Deuteronomy 17:14-20

V. 14: When you come to the land which the Lord your God is giving you, and possess it and dwell in it, and say, "I will set a king over me like all the nations that are around me."

V. 15: you shall surely set a king over you whom the Lord your God chooses; one from your brethren from among your brethren you shall set as king over you; you may not set a foreigner over you, who is not your brother.

V. 16: But he shall not multiply horses for himself, nor cause the people to return to Egypt to multiply horses, for the Lord has said to you, "You shall not return that way again."

V. 17: Neither shall he multiply wives for himself, lest his heart turn away, nor shall he greatly multiply silver and gold for himself.

V. 18: Also it shall be, when he sets on the throne of his kingdom, that he shall write for himself a copy of this law in a book, from the one before the priests, the Levites.

V. 19: And it shall be with him, and he shall read it all the days of his life, that he may learn to fear the Lord his God and be careful to observe all the words of this law, and these statutes.

V. 20: that his heart may not be lifted above his brethren, that he may not turn aside from the commandment to the right hand or-to the left, and that he might prolong his days in his kingdom, he and his children in the midst of Israel.

1 Kings 11:1-13

V. 1: But King Solomon loved many foreign women, as well as the daughter of Pharaoh: women of the Moabites, Ammonites, Edomites, Sidonians, and Hittites

V. 2: from the nations of whom the Lord had said to the children of Israel, "You shall not intermarry with them, nor they with you. Surely they will turn away your hearts to their gods." Solomon clung to these in love.

V. 3: And he had seven hundred wives, princesses, and three hundred concubines; and his wives turned away his heart.

V. 4: For it was so, that when Solomon was old, that his wives turned his heart towards other gods; and his heart was not loyal to the Lord his

God, as was the heart of his father David.

V. 5: For Solomon went after Ashtoreth the goddess of the Sidonians, and after Milcom the abomination of the Ammonites

V. 6: Solomon did evil in the sight of the Lord, and did not fully follow the Lord as did his father David.

V. 7: Then Solomon built a high place for Chemosh the abomination of Moab, on a hill that is east of Jerusalem, and for Molech the abomination of the people of Ammon.

V. 8: And he did likewise for all his foreign wives, who burned incense and sacrificed to their gods.

V. 9: So the Lord became angry with Solomon, because his heart had turned from the Lord God of Israel, who had appeared to him twice.

V. 10: and had commanded him concerning this thing, that he should not go after other gods; but he did not keep what the Lord had commanded.

V. 11: Therefore the Lord said to Solomon, "Because you have done this, and have not kept my covenant and my statutes, which I have commanded you, I will surely tear the kingdom away from you and give It to your servant.

V. 12: Nevertheless I will not do it in your days, for the sake of your father David; I will tear it out of the hand of your son.

V. 13: However I will not tear away the whole kingdom: I will give one tribe to your son for the sake of my servant David, and for the sake of Jerusalem which I have chosen.

Read 1 Kings 12

2 Chronicles 15:2: And he went out to meet Asa, and said to him, hear me Asa and all Judah and Benjamin, The Lord is with you while you are with Him. If you seek Him, He will be found by You; but if you forsake Him, He will forsake you.

2 Chronicles 31:21: And in every work that he began in the service of the house of God, in the law and in the commandment to seek his God, he did it with all his heart. So he prospered.

2 Chronicles 32:25: But Hezekiah did not repay according to the favor shown him, for his heart was lifted up; therefore wrath was looming over him and over Judah and

Jerusalem.

V. 26: The Hezekiah humbled himself for the pride of his heart, he and the inhabitants of Jerusalem, so that the wrath of the Lord did not come upon them in the days of Hezekiah

2 Chronicles 33: 9-19
V. 9: So Manasseh seduced Judah and the inhabitants of Jerusalem to do more evil than the nations whom the Lord had destroyed before the children of Israel.
V. 10: And the Lord spoke to Manasseh and his people, but they would not listen.
V. 11: Therefore, the Lord brought upon them the captains of the army of the king of Assyria, who took Manasseh with hooks, bound him with bronze fetters, and carried him off to Babylon.
V. 12: Now when he was in affliction, he implored the Lord his God, and humbled himself greatly before the God of his fathers,
V. 13: and prayed to him; and he received his entreaty, heard his supplication, and brought him back to Jerusalem into his kingdom. Then Manasseh knew that the Lord was God.
V. 14: After this he built a wall outside the city of David on the west side of Gihon, in the valley, as far as the entrance to the Fish Gate; and it enclosed Opel, and he raised it to a great height. Then he put military captains in all the fortified cities of Judah.
V. 15: He took away the foreign gods and the idol from the house of the Lord, and all the alters that he had built in the mount of the house of the Lord and in Jerusalem; and he cast them out of the city.
V. 16: He also repaired the altar of the Lord, sacrificed peace offerings and thank offerings on it, and commanded Judah to serve-the Lord God of Israel.
V. 17: Nevertheless the people still sacrificed on the high places, but only to the Lord their God.
V. 18: Now the rest of the acts of Manasseh, his prayer to his God, and the words of his seers who spoke to him in the name of the Lord God of Israel, indeed they are written in book of the kings of Israel.
V. 19: Also his prayer and how God received his entreaty, and all his sin and trespass, and the site where he built high places and set up wooden images and carved images, before he was humbled, indeed they are written among the sayings of Hozai.

2 Chronicles 36:12-16

V. 12: He did evil in the sight of the Lord his God, and did not humble himself before Jeremiah the prophet, who spake from the mouth of Lord.

V. 13: And he also rebelled against king Nebuchadnezzar, who had made him swear an oath by God; but he stiffened his neck and hardened his heart against turning to the Lord God of Israel.

V. 14: Moreover all the leaders of the priests and the people transgressed more and more, according to all the abominations of the nations, and defiled the house of the Lord which he had consecrated in Jerusalem.

V. 15: And the Lord God of their fathers sent warnings to them by His messengers, rising up early and sending them, because He had compassion on His people and on His dwelling place.

V. 16: But they mocked the messengers of God, despised His words, and scoffed at His prophets, until the wrath of Lord arose against His people, till there was no remedy.

1 Kings 13:33-34

V. 33: After this event Jeroboam did not turn from his evil way, but again he made priests from every class of people from the high places; whoever wished, he consecrated him, and he became one of the priests of the high places.

V. 34: And this thing was the sin of the house of Jeroboam, so as to exterminate and destroy it from the face of the earth.

2 Kings 17:16-18

V. 16: So they left the commandments of the Lord their God, made for themselves a molded image of two calves, made a wooden image and worshipped all the host of heaven, and saved Baal.

V. 17: And they caused their sons and daughters to pass through the fire, practiced witchcraft and soothsaying, and sold themselves to do evil in the sight of the Lord, to provoke Him to anger.

V. 18: Therefore the Lord was very angry with Israel, and removed them from His sight; there was none left but the tribe of Judah alone.

2 Kings 25:22: Then he made Gedaliah the son of Ahikam, the son of Shaphan, governor over the people who remained in the land of Judah, whom Nebuchadnezzar king of Babylon had left.

1 Chronicles 3:10-19

2 Chronicles 36:3, 10
V. 3: Now the king of Egypt deposed him at Jerusalem, and he imposed on the land a tribute of one hundred talents of silver and a talent of gold.
V. 10: At the turn of the year king Nebuchadnezzar summoned him and took him to Babylon, with the costly articles from the house of the Lord, and made Zedekiah, "Jehoiakim's brother, king over Judah and Jerusalem.

Charismatic Leaders of the Old Testament

Numbers 12:6-8
V. 6
>Then He said, "Hear now my words:
>If there is a prophet among you,
>I, the Lord, make myself known to you
>in a vision I speak to him in a dream.

V. 7
>Not so with my servant
>Moses He is faithful in all my house

V. 8
>I speak with him face to face
>Even plainly, and not in dark sayings
>And he sees the form of the Lord
>Why then were you not afraid
>To speak against My servant Moses

Acts 7:23-29
V. 23: Now when he was forty years old, it came into his heart to visit his brethren, the children of Israel.
V. 24: And seeing one of them suffer wrong, he defended and avenged him who was oppressed, and struck down the Egyptian.
V. 25: For he supposed that his brethren would have understood that God would deliver them by his hand, but they did not understand.
V. 26: And the next day he appeared to two of them as they were fighting, and tried to reconcile them, saying, "Men, you are brethren; why do you wrong one another?"
V. 27: But he who did his neighbor wrong pushed him away, saying, Who

made you a ruler and a judge over us?
- V. 28: Do you want to kill me as you did the Egyptian yesterday?
- V. 29: Then, at this saying, Moses fled and became a dweller in the land of Midian, where he had two sons.

Exodus 4:29-31
- V. 29: Then Moses and Aaron went and gathered together all the elders of the children of Israel.
- V. 30: And Aaron spoke all the words which the Lord had spoken to Moses. Then he did the signs in the sight of the people.
- V. 31: So the people believed; and when they heard that the Lord had visited the children of Israel and that He had looked on their affliction, then they bowed their heads and worshipped.

Exodus 16

Numbers 12-13

Exodus 16:7-8
- V. 7: And in the morning you shall see the glory of the Lord; for He hears your complaints against the Lord. But what are we, that you complain against us?
- V. 8: Also Moses said, "This shall be seen when the Lord gives you meat to eat in the evening, and in the morning bread to the full; for the Lord hears your complaints which you make against Him. And what are we? Your complaints are not against us but against the Lord:"

Numbers 20:12: Then the Lord spoke to Moses and Aaron, "Because you did not believe Me, to hallow Me in the eyes of the children of Israel, therefore you shall not bring this assembly into the land which I have given them."

Deuteronomy 31:1-8
- V. 1: Then Moses went and spoke these words to the people.
- V. 2: And he said to them: I am one hundred and twenty years old today, I can no longer go out and come in. Also the Lord has said to me, 'You shall not cross over this Jordan.'
- V. 3: The Lord your God Himself crosses over before you; He will destroy these nations from before you and you shall dispossess them. Joshua himself crosses over before you, just as the Lord has said.

V. 4: And the Lord will do to them as He did to Sihon and Og, the kings of the Amorites and their land, when He destroyed them.

V. 5: The Lord will give them over to you, that you may do to them according to every commandment which I have commanded you.

V. 6: Be strong and of good courage, do not fear or be afraid of them; for the Lord your God, He is one who goes with you. He will not leave you nor forsake you

V. 7: Then Moses called Joshua and said to him in the sight of all Israel, "Be strong and of good courage, for you must go with this people to the land which the Lord has sworn to their fathers to give them, and you shall cause them to inherit it.

V. 8: And the Lord, He is the one who goes before you. He will be with you, He will not leave you nor forsake you; do not fear nor be dismayed."

Joshua 1:2-9

V. 2: Moses My servant is dead. Now therefore arise go over this Jordan, you and all this people, to the land which I am giving to them-the children of Israel.

V. 3: Every place that the sole of your foot will tread upon I have given you, as I said to Moses.

V. 4: From the wilderness and this Lebanon as far as the great river, the River Euphrates, all the land of the Hittites, and to the great sea toward the going down of the sun, shall be your territory.

V. 5: No man shall be able to stand before you all the days of your life; as I was with Moses, so I will be with you. I will not leave you nor-forsake you.

V. 6: Be strong and of good courage, for to this people you shall divide as an inheritance the land which I swore to their fathers to give them.

V. 7: Only be strong and very courageous, that you may observe to do according to all the law which Moses my servant commanded you; do not turn from it to the right or to the left, that you may prosper wherever you go.

V. 8: This Book of the law shall not depart from your mouth, but you shall meditate in it day and night, that you may observe to do according to all that is written in it. For then you will make your way prosperous, and then you will have good success.

V. 9: Have I not commanded you? Be strong and of good courage; do not be afraid, nor be dismayed, for the Lord your God is with you wherever you go.

Judges 2:16:	Nevertheless, the Lord raised up judges who delivered them out of the hands who plundered them.
Judges 10:7:	So the anger of the Lord was hot against Israel; and He sold them into the hands of the Philistines and into the hands of the people of Ammon.

Judges 3:9, 15
V. 9:   When the children of Israel cried out to the Lord, the Lord raised up a deliverer for the children of Israel, who delivered them: Othniel the son of Kenaz, Caleb's younger brother.
V. 15: But when the children of Israel cried out to the Lord, the Lord raised up a deliverer for them: Ehud the son of Gera, the Benjamite, a left-handed man. By him the children of Israel sent tribute to Eglon king of Moab.

Judges 3:10:	The Spirit of the Lord came upon him, and he judged Israel. He went out to war, and the Lord delivered Cushan-Rishathaim king of Mesopotamia into his hand; and his hand prevailed over Cushan-Rishathaim
6:34:	But the Spirit of the Lord came upon Gideon; then he blew the trumpet, and the Abiezrites gathered behind him.
11:29:	Then the Spirit of the Lord came upon Jephthah, -and he passed through Gilead and Manasseh, and passed through Mizpah and Gilead; and from Mizpah of Gilead he advanced toward the people of Ammon.
Judges 13:25:	And the Spirit of the Lord began to move upon him at Mahaneh Dan between Zorah and Eshtaol.

Judges 14:6, 19
V. 6:   And the Spirit of the Lord came mightily upon him, and he tore the lion apart as one would have torn apart a young goat, though he had nothing in his hands. But he did not tell his father or mother what he had done.

V. 19: Then the Spirit of the Lord came upon him mightily, and he went down to Ashkelon and killed thirty of their men, took their apparel, and gave pieces of clothing to those who had explained the riddle. So his anger was aroused, and he went back up to his father's house

15:14 When he came to Lehi, the Philistines came shouting against him. Then the Spirit of the Lord came mightily upon him; and the ropes that were on his arms became like flax that was burned with fire, and his bonds broke loose from his hands.

Jeremiah 18:18: Then they said, "Come and let us devise plans against Jeremiah; for the law shall not perish from the priests, nor counsel from the wise, nor the word from the prophet. Come and let us attack him with the tongue, and let us not give heed to any of his words.

1 Chronicles 27:32-33
V. 32: Also Jehonathan, David's uncle, was a counselor, a wise man, and a scribe; and Jehiel the son of Hachmoni was with the King's sons.
V. 33: Ahithophel was the king's counselor, and Hushai the Archite was the king's companion.

Exodus 4:16: So he shall be your spokesman to the people. And he himself shall be a mouth for you, and you shall be to him as God.

2 Kings 8

Religious Leaders of the Old Testament with Scripture References

Exodus 19:6: And you shall be to Me a kingdom of priests and a Holy nation. These are the words which you shall speak to the children of Israel.

Read Leviticus 8

Exodus 28:2, 36
V. 2: And you shall make holy garments for Aaron and your brother, for

glory and beauty.

V. 36: You shall make a plate of pure gold and engrave on it, like the engraving of a signet: HOLINESS TO THE LORD.

Read: Leviticus 21, 22:9

Numbers 27:21: He shall stand before Eleazar the priest, who shall inquire before the Lord for him by the judgment of the Urim. At his word they shall go out, and at his word they shall come in, he and all the children of Israel with him-all the congregations."

Leviticus 10:10-11
V. 10: that you may distinguish between holy and unholy, and between clean and unclean.
V. 11: and that you may teach the children of Israel all the statutes which the Lord has spoken to them by the hand of Moses.

Exodus 32:26: then Moses stood in the entrance of the camp, and said, "Whoever is on the Lord's side come to me come to me!" And all the sons of Levi gathered themselves together to him.

Numbers 8:14-19
V. 14: Thus you shall separate the Levites from among the children of Israel and the Levites shall be mine.
V. 15: After that the Levites shall go in to service the tabernacle of meeting. So you shall cleanse them and offer them like a wave offering.
V. 16: for they are wholly given to Me from among the children of Israel; I have taken them for Myself instead of all who open the womb, the first born of all the children of Israel.
V. 17: For all the firstborn among the children of Israel are mine, both man and beast; on the day that I struck all the firstborn in the land of Egypt I sanctified them to Myself.
V. 18: I have taken the Levites instead of all the firstborn 0f the children of Israel.
V 19: and I have given the Levites as a gift to Aaron and his sons from among the children of Israel, to do the work for the children of Israel in the tabernacle of meeting, and to make atonement for the children of Israel, that there be no plague among the children of Israel when

the children of Israel come near the sanctuary."

Numbers 4:3:	From thirty years old and above, even to fifty years old, all who enter the service to do the work in the tabernacle of meeting.
Numbers 1:53:	But the Levites shall camp around the tabernacle of the testimony, that there may be no wrath on the congregation of the children of Israel; and the Levites shall keep charge of the tabernacle of the testimony.
Numbers 3:28:	According to the number of all the males, from a month old and above, there were eight thousand six hundred keeping charge of the sanctuary.
8:19:	And I have given the Levites as a gift to Aaron and his sons from among the children of Israel, to do the work of the children of Israel in the tabernacle of meeting, and to make atonement for the children of Israel, that there be no plaque among the children of Israel when the children of Israel come near the sanctuary."

We Come Now to the New Testament

In New Testament times, there were no longer the civil leaders of the Old Testament theocracy. Now there were official religious leaders, but their office was no longer hereditary. And there were charismatic religious leaders, though none of these bore the prominence of the prophets or statesmen of the Old Testament. This may be explained by the fact that the official leaders were to be chosen on recognition of their godliness and gifts, quite a different system than the Old Testament priesthood. The Jewish priesthood continued in into New Testament times, but the church and its government evolved outside Judaism. In fact, the New Testament seems to have resisted using clerical words for their ministries.

Religious Leaders

The twelve apostles were chosen not in recognition of special spiritual endowment but solely on Jesus' initiative. Their purpose was to be with Him and then to go out and preach (Mark 3:14) and to do miracles (Matt. 10:7). After the ascension, those twelve who had been closest to Jesus during His life now became His representatives, assuming an authoritative position in the company of Christians. New converts early came under their teaching ministry (Acts 2:42) miracles continued of signs and wonders (Acts 5:12; 2 Cor. 12:12). They were overseers of the administration of funds (Acts 4:37) until they needed help and the job was transferred to others (Acts 6: 1-6). They exercised discipline on occasion (Acts 5:1-11) and likely led in the celebration of the Lord's Supper. When problems arose, they took the lead in solving those problems along with the elders. With the church expanding into other areas, their attention was on those groups as well (Acts 8:14, 9:32; Gal. 1:19) assumes that most of them are out of town (Jerusalem) on missionary work. Their commitment was to the congregation of believers not to Peter.

The replacement of Judas was chosen by the casting of lots under the direction of the Holy Spirit and also with the qualifications of being an eyewitness from John's baptism tell the ascension (Acts 1:21-22) after this no efforts were made to select successors for those who died (Acts 12: 2).

As the apostles and missionary prophets and teachers died off or moved on, there was left a need for someone to be the focal point for the community life of the local group of believers. These leaders were referred to as elders (presbuteroi) and overseers/bishops (episkopoi) Paul spoke to the Ephesian elders to shepherd the flock over which God's Spirit had made them overseers (Acts 20:28), yet in v. 17 they are called elders. Their status was "elder," and their job was to oversee.

The elders are first mentioned in Acts 11:30. In the narrative concerning the council in Jerusalem they are always named in conjunction with the apostles as the decision makers (Acts 15:2, 4, 6, 22, 23). They functioned as a supreme court for the entire church. Out beyond Jerusalem elders were appointed in the churches founded by Paul and Barnabas, already on their first missionary journey (Acts 14:23; Titus 1:5-9).

The bishop was a distinct office that one might seek (1Tim. 3:1), and that was to be done voluntarily and eagerly not for gain. The qualifications were listed but not the duties. Moral reliability came first. The overseer needed to live an honorable and exemplary life, avoiding excesses. Then there must be proof in his own home of his ability to lead the life of the congregation; high value was placed on a well ordered and hospitable home. The overseer should be an apt teacher. He must be mature and not susceptible to pride, which comes all too natural to those who do well. Finally, he must be above reproach according to the standards of the non-Christian world so as to be kept away from scandal. In the first mention of deacons (Phil. 1:1). We find them linked with the overseers and mentioned after them. Their qualifications are mentioned in 1 Timothy 3 after those of the overseers. While many qualifications are the same for both, we see evidence that the two offices are different, the deacon need not be apt to teach, but should not be double tongued or greedy, qualities very apt for those who visit in many homes and who have the administration of funds. Their capacity to serve as deacons was a gift from God (1 Cor. 12:28). Their function seems to carry out the original meaning of their name (didaskein, "to wait at tables") as it is used in (Acts 6:2) there the twelve led the congregation to select seven men for that job (though Stephen and Philip at least were also known as preachers and teachers of the word). The church seems to use this term to express generally the same love and care for others. In the early Jerusalem church the apostles yet carried out the function that would be taken up by the overseers/elders, and accordingly the need for deacons become the first obvious vacancy in church community leadership.

Understand your work and role as a deacon, because now that you are a deacon there is great work for you to do. I hope that you feel God's energy flowing through you. My wish for you is that you experience a sense of divine purpose as Jesus did when He said, "I must be about my Father's business." And feel the thrill of service as Paul when he said, "For this day I was born!" You can find no happier person than the individual who is busy for the master, using his gifts in Christian service. Though spoken to his weary troops, the words of George Washington seem to prevent a special challenge for deacons and other Christians and leaders alike, "The fate of unborn millions may now depend, under God, upon the conduct and courage of this army. We cannot fail as Christians and leaders; the morality of our country depends on us.

God give me work, till my life shall end, and life till my work is done.

Along with deacons there were also deaconnessess. The first mentioned is Phoebe (Romans 16:1).

Charismatic Leaders

In the New Testament, there is not a dean description between official leaders and charismatic leaders for the office was by the very nature if it intended for persons who were recognized for, among other qualifications, their spiritual gifts.

Though prophets ranked in importance second only to (1 Cor. 12:28-31; Eph. 4:11) none carried the role of statesmen as did Samuel, Elijah, Isaiah, and Jeremiah. The prophet's ministry included revelation (1 Cor. 14:29-32), predictions, identifying individuals for specific ministry (Acts 13:1-3), and bestowing on them the spiritual gifts that would enable them to carry out their tasks (1 Tim. 4:14). Prophecy was intended for the edification, exhortation, and consolation of the church community (1 Cor. 14:3; Acts 15:32).

Theological Dimensions of Leadership in the Bible

The scripture indicates there is no authority except what God has established (Rom. 13:1). He sets over us whom He wishes (Dan. 4:32, 5:21) to be His minister to us. Moses and Joshua were assigned their leadership by God (Exod. 4; Josh. 1). Aaron and his sons were singled out for the priesthood (Exod. 28:1). The judges were raised up by God (Judg. 2:16). Saul was appointed by the Lord (1 Sam. 10:1); David and his line were chosen by God (1 Sam. 13:14; 2 Sam. 7). The prophets were called of God, like the apostles.

The capacity to serve in the church is described as a gift from God (1 Car. 12:28). Promotions come neither from the East or West but from the Lord. He puts down one and sets up another (Ps. 75:6-7).

The role of leadership was not intended for our advantage -but for service (Luke 22:26). Accordingly, Israel's kings were not to lift themselves above their countrymen (Deut. 17:20). Paul saw his apostleship as a call of sacrificial labor rather than his own glory (1 Cor. 15:9-10). The elders were to shepherd the flock to sacrificially care for the souls of the faithful, giving account to God (Heb. 13:17; 1 Peter 5:2-3). Gifts were to be used in serving one another as stewards of God's Grace (1 Pet. 4:10). When Korah was not content to serve in a secondary role of leadership appointed him, he was rebuked and judged (Num. 16:9-33). James and John likewise needed to learn the humility of serving (Mark 10:35-45). Leaders are accountable to God (Heb. 13:17). To whom much has been given will much be required (Luke 12:48) is nowhere more evident than in Moses's disobedience at Maribah (Num. 20:12). The same was applied to teachers in the New Testament (James 3:1).

Leaders in Our Day

Today, we face problems that seem too big to handle. The moral decay of our country is rampant; our moral standards are almost forgotten. Our youth, the future of our country, are alienated and confused. Our country is financially troubled. The stability of our economy gets worse each day, but still the most serious problem we have today is effective leadership.

The things that have created this void are our lack of positive, creative, constructive and motivated leadership training. There are very few leadership qualities being exercised today. These crises have been the result of staying away from the standards this country was founded on. Our youth is -the most valuable asset we have; this means we must find those youth with leadership qualities and develop them for the future of our country.

We can watch the rise and fall of any organization by the quality of their leadership. Strong, dedicated leadership is imperative to the success of any group, be it government, secular, industry, or our churches.

It has been pointed out that business leaders are the basic and scarcest resource of any business enterprise. In other words, the power of leadership seems to be declining everywhere. More and more of the men we see coming to the top seem to merely be drifting. The result is helplessness in a collective leadership that hides from the public.

In every area of our country today, we are starving for strong and effective leadership, not only in our churches, but also in public life as well-government, business, education, and industry; we need teamwork.

The effective leader doesn't wait for things to happen; he makes things happen, he takes the initiative.

There is no lack of people to fill the administrative positions, but the commitment in leadership is not there. In today's society, there are too few individuals to manage the changes and at the same time exercise the leadership qualities and commitment needed to follow through.

Leadership experience of any kind is important, but there is no such thing as a born leader. Some have more leadership qualities than others and are more easily developed. Leadership is more than just being in charge you must be qualified you must know your industry. You must be good in human relations, and you must learn human nature; this is a learned process. It's always under construction.

The Christian organizations must strive to set leadership standards, for the non-Christian in all areas of leadership. The Christian must operate on the assumption that they are a part of something and are doing something that has eternal value. The Christian organizations must set higher values on individual and personal development needs.

A Christian organization is made up of mostly volunteers. It is not always a difficult thing to lead people who depend on an organization for their livelihood. The Christian organization must have excellent leaders, because the people they lead and motivate are 98 percent volunteers. So we need to focus on leadership training, for it is up to the leaders to motivate and get the group to function properly.

We must have a clear understanding of the nature of leadership, and to accomplish this we borrow from the secular research and analysis scripture to acquire an adequate Christian philosophy of leadership to guide Christian enterprises into the area of success.
Are you involved in a Christian organization that's going nowhere? Are you involved in an area of industry with desired results it can't achieve?

You may have a fixed objective to serve Christ or any number of things, too often the reason things come to a dead end is because the objectives or goals are not dearly defined. To be an effective leader, you must know what your objectives or goals are. When you see leader in this material, it singles out one who leads, who takes charge, one who guides, directs, and develops others in their activities and seeks to provide continual training in all areas.

Today, there are two kinds of people, there are leaders and there are followers. Leadership is a perfectly natural thing; when things move it is because of effective leadership. We have put this material together in hopes that it will quicken your spirits to accept the challenges, to strive toward the qualities that go into better leadership. We as leaders in either the Christian or secular areas must understand in what area of the leadership role we belong. To be a leader in industry, a company must have innovation. Small firms produce about four times as many innovative ideas per dollar as medium-size firms and about twenty-four times that of large firms, which shows leadership on the part of the small firms. We must be creative in our efforts.

Leadership is many things. It is having patience. It is being there when things go bad, not being in the way when things go well. It is listening carefully at all times. It is speaking with encouragement and reinforcing words with action. A leader's responsibility is to wake up the creativity in others. A leader is primarily an expert in the promotion and protection of values.

Probably the most important management fundamental that is being ignored today is staying dose to the customer to satisfy his/her needs and anticipate his/her wants. In too many companies, the customers have become a nuisance whose unpredictable behavior damages carefully made strategic plans, whose activities mess up computer operations, and who stubbornly insists that purchased products should work.

Management. To understand the process of delegation (managing by getting results effectively through others), one must understand the concept of responsibility, authority, and accountability. Although a manager cannot delegate ultimate responsibility, he/she can delegate authority. It is through the combination of sharing responsibility through assignment and delegating authority that a manager can hold other levels accountable for getting things done.

Functions of Management

1. Planning. This function consists of forecasting future events and determining the most effective future activities for the company.
2. Organizing. This function consists of ways in which the organizational structure is established and how authority and responsibilities are given to managers, a task called delegation.
3. Commanding. This function is concerned how managers direct employees. Such activities have been addressed as effective communications, managerial behavior, and the uses of rewards and punishments in discussing how a manager should command employees.
4. Coordinating. This function is concerned with activities designed to create a relationship between all the organizations efforts (individual tasks) to accomplish a common goal.
5. Controlling. This function is concerned as to how the manager evaluates performance within the organization in relationship to the plans and goals of the organization.

Principles of Management

1. Division of Labor. Work is separated into its basic tasks and divided between individual workers or work groups that can specialize in the specific task, leading to work specialization.
2. Authority. Authority is the legitimate right to exercise power within the organization to obtain worker obedience. It is closely related to responsibility, which is the accountability for using authority. Authority and responsibility go together; one without the other leads to managerial failure.
3. Discipline. Discipline is the application of punishment for failure to act in accord with those who possess legitimate authority in the organization.
4. Unity of Command. Each worker should receive orders from only one manager, a simplified view of an organization that assures a minimum of conflict and promotes clarity of communications.

5. Unity of Direction. The whole organization should have only one goal and seek to accomplish that goal in all activities.

6. Subordination of the Individual. The goals and interests of the organization are more important than and therefore take precedence over the personal goals and interests of the individual.

7. Compensation. Each employee should receive compensation in accord with a general formula that is applied to all. The compensation of amounts and forms of compensation should consider the following variables: cost of living, the general economic climate and specific business conditions, qualifications of the worker and the supply and demand for such worker, and the level of productivity achieved.

8. Centralization. The importance of subordinates is reduced as organizational power and the responsibility for decision making is concentrated in managers. Managers are responsible for decision making and are accountable for those decisions. Subordinates should be delegated with enough responsibility and authority to accomplish the assigned task. The opposite of centralization is decentralization.

9. Chain of Command. Authority and responsibility are delegated down the chain of command. Lower-level managers have the responsibility of informing those seniors in the chain of command of current information regarding accomplished tasks.

10. Orders. The resources of a company. Its raw materials and workers must be in the right place at the right time. This ordering of organizational resources ensures maximal efficiency.

11. Equity. Employees should feel they are being treated equally and fairly. The prescription of equity will be accomplished by organizational rules that are reasonable and consistently applied to all workers.

12. Stability of Personnel. Successful firms retain good managers, and this should be a goal of the organization. Skilled and successful personnel are vital organizational resources, and organizational practice should encourage long-term commitment to the organization.

13. Initiative. Management should encourage individual employee initiative, which is defined as additional self-motivated work efforts undertaken for the good of the organization.

14. Esprit de Corps; Harmony. Management should encourage harmony and common interests, resulting in good relations among employees.

Some Key Terms of Management

1. Management. Working with and through others to accomplish the objective of both the organization and its members.

2. Responsibility. The duty or task to be performed.

3. Authority. The power to act for someone else.

Management Activities. Includes planning, organizing, staffing, coordinating, motivating, leading, controlling; getting results effectively through other people by process of delegation.

Technical Activities. The specialist's functions of an individual or those that derive from his/her vocational fields.

Accountability. The obligation to be held responsible for what was expected or what happened that was unexpected.

The functions of management, principles of management, and management activities are here to give you an idea of some of the differences in the two: leadership and management.

A good leader must be strong in both managerial and decision-making qualities in order to motivate people into action. The good leader will always be able to make a swift decision without hesitation. (Motivation is a process of stimulating an individual to take action that will accomplish a desired goal.) Motivational practices have been with us for a long time.

Highly motivated individuals can bring about increased productivity, job satisfaction, a decrease in absenteeism, grievances, etc. So based on these conditions, it is important for us to study motivation. Motivation can be described as a process of stimulating an individual to take action that will lead to fulfillment of a need or the accomplishment of a desired goal.

There are many theories of motivation. The traditional one is that money is-the primary motivator. If financial rewards are great enough, workers will produce more. So in this case, financial rewards should be related to performance.

It has also been suggested that only unsatisfied needs are primary sources for motivation. So only if you have an intense craving to succeed, you will study and learn as much as you can in order to fulfill this ambition.

Another suggestion is that there are five needs that motivate: (1) survival, (2) safety or security, (3) a sense of belonging, (4) ego status, (5) self-satisfaction.

You should remember the factors chat motivate people change at different stages of life, for example, when first married, when nearing retirement.

But many studies have found surprising similarities in how people rank these factors most important to them. Respect is close to the top always; employment is also at the top of basic needs.

Leadership is behavioral requirements to meet its goals. There must be an influence to direct toward a desired result. We, as leaders, lead in many different directions. Just because we have high positions according to our jobs does not mean that we are leaders, or even with certain personal characteristics. There are very few who can meet every situation or requirement.

We must realize that faith people are people of action. You must have fifth to have leadership. When God creates a leader, he is a man of action (Phil. 2: 13). This is how God works in people; prayer is not a substitute for action. When God motivates people, it does not mean their actions are inactive, this is not biblical. For Paul to get results in his ministry he had to act (1 Cor. 15:10). God depends on us to act (1 Sam. 2:3). In 2 Timothy 4:7, Paul was able to say I have fought a good fight, meaning that grace was very evident in his life. But as an agent, he had to act to have that kind of leadership. Paul was a leader by example; by this we mean that he used Jesus Christ as his example.

Professionals are the best at what they do, and they get results. So we need to enlarge the definition of leadership. Leaders should be considered professionals. People are where they are because of credentials of prescribed study more than because they perform competently; otherwise, they lose their right to practice through competition.

To get the best results, a leader must act decisively and follow certain principles. Here are some consideration to achieve best results:

1. Objectives. Decide the desired results you want to accomplish. Put it in writing, clearly, accurately, and fully inform your people.

2. Activities. Determine the major activities to be performed to achieve your goals. Short-, mid-, and long-term goals, be specific. Make sure every activity is necessary. This is important to achieve end results.

3. Timetable. Set up work schedules. Make sure there is a timetable for every step's completion. Do not stray from your schedule or change it; make sure you utilize all your time and follow through.

4. Controls. Decide where your desired viewpoints of progress are. Make only necessary adjustments.

5. Responsibilities. Make sure all responsibilities are assigned and make sure it is coordinated and controlled.

6. Communications. Keep everyone involved fully informed. Your people must keep you advised on all pertinent matters if you are to be successful. The more informed they are, the easier it is to accomplish the task.

7. Cooperation. Any task we attempt to accomplish must have complete cooperation. There must not be any misunderstanding or loose motions. Everything must be clear in the beginning; friction undoubtedly delays progress.

8. Problem Solving. Handle each problem as it comes up, but don't put it off tackle one problem at a time. Decide on a plan of action and act. Check results periodically to see what improvements there are act and follow through.

9. Credit. Make sure any person involved in these areas in any way are acknowledged for their efforts.

Although leadership has distinctive characteristics, it is an attitude of actions. There is a difference between leadership and management.

1. Leadership exercises faith. Management deals with facts.

2. Leadership provides direction. Management is concerned with control.

Most leaders fail because they do not have the capacity to take right and necessary actions.

Leadership and Management Compared

Leadership	Management
1. Is quality	1. Is a science and an art
2. Provides vision	2. Supplies a realistic perspective
3. Deals with concepts	3. Relates to functions
4. Exercises faith	4. Deals with facts
5. Seeks effectiveness	5. Strives for efficiency
6. Is an influence for good among potential resources	6. Is the coordination of available resources organized for maximum accomplishments
7. Provides direction	7. Is concerned with control
8. Thrives on finding opportunity	8. Succeeds on accomplishments

A leader from this book is one who acts and performs these activities, one who guides others to accomplish their task He has the capacity to develop the potential into a profitable and practical means. He has the faith and ability to accomplish and acts on that fact. The true leader must have the initiative and drive to see that whatever the task might be could be completed.

In Exodus 18:25, Moses chose able men out of all Israel and made them heads over the people, rulers over thousands, hundreds, fifties, and tens. Leadership represents action. But it is also a set of tools. Effective leadership can be used for worldly purposes by people who are not spiritual at all; on the other hand, spiritual men can take these same tools and use them for God's glory. It doesn't make any difference whether he is spiritual or not.

Where should men look for these tools? Should we borrow from the secular world? Is leadership a biblical concept? Are there valid principles for organizations and spiritual leadership? Are there methods in the Bible to guide our thinking as we study? Yes, absolutely, as we allow ourselves to have an open mind to perceive its insights. I believe that every basic foundation of honorable principles in leadership and management are found in the Bible. As people God chose met His Spiritual requirements, they were used to their full limits despite their human shortcomings.

The leaders in the Old Testament had some failures at one time or another. But the key to their success was that they never quit. They learned from their failures, repented, and used it as stepping stones to bigger achievements through God's direction.

Let us stimulate the thoughtful person to further study by using a few Old Testament passages:

Joseph. What an excellent example of leadership. Look at Genesis 41 where Joseph was restored to power by pharaoh after the interpretation of the dream. Joseph was made second in command. Joseph allowed God to take control of his leadership qualities. What an example of leadership and organization. God did not simply put these skills in Joseph's mind. I believe God will direct all of us to the subject we need to study, if we will use those qualities.

The perspective of leadership must be based on our perspective of man. Look at Isaial1 53:6, all we, like sheep, have gone astray; we have turned everyone to his own way. So you see, we must have leaders to direct our way. People need direction so as to be directed toward one common goal.

God has ordained direction from the scripture. Look at Exodus 18:13-27.

Jethro's advice to Moses caused him to set up lines of authority. In this we see the art of delegation of responsibility as well as authority. To be a good leader, you must be able to delegate responsibility and authority, enough to accomplish the task at hand. Whenever possible, these responsibilities should be stated in writing. The follower should also have a good idea of how the job fits into the total picture and why it is important. The leader should also encourage questions and be completely approachable. This practice, in combination with exhibiting confidence and trust by allowing followers to pursue goals without undue reporting, constant checking, and other exaggerated forms of control, will create a supportive climate and help to build an effective working relationship.

Performance

Once the followers understand the job, they should be made aware of how performance will be measured. Leaders receive the type and level of job performance they expect within reason over a period of time. In fact, low expectations tend to breed low performance, and the opposite is true of high expectations. The failure to confront lower than desired levels of performance is to acknowledge them as acceptable, high expectations mean setting challenging but achievable goals. The focus should be on results that are motivated and attainable.

The leader should establish a system for setting objectives and a procedure for periodically reporting progress toward these objectives. Consideration of less-experienced followers demands more frequent consultation and reporting. The leader who is committed to delegating authority should avoid switching back and forth in delegation, because it will only cause confusion and stagnation among followers.

Limitations

It may seem self-evident, but delegation cannot be used when the follower does not welcome additional responsibility. Knowing who wants greater responsibility or a promotion is as important as knowing who is qualified for a job. It is often difficult for successful leaders, who owe their success to a driving desire for greater responsibility and recognition to understand others who seem to lack that motivation.

The leader-follower relationship is one of interdependence. A major goal of delegation is to reduce dependence on the leader, but the leader has a certain responsibility for helping the follower discover how best to develop his/her abilities in order to meet future responsibilities.

Leaders can develop followers or future leaders through the art of delegation and should practice this art judiciously. With effective delegation, a leader can multiply his/her effectiveness and through others achieve the results expected.

An important principle here is that authority should equal the responsibility. This is known as equal authority and responsibility and insures that work will be performed with a minimum amount of frustration on the part of the followers. But not delegating authority equal to the responsibility, a leader will create employee dissatisfaction and generally waste energies and resources.

Chain of Command

This means that there should be a dear definition of authority in the organization and that authority flows one link at a time, through the chain of command from top to bottom of the organization. Communication in the organization is through channels. Following this procedure, there will be results in clarification of relationships, less confusion, and improved decision making. Remember, understanding the process of delegation involves employing the principles of responsibility, authority, and accountability, as well as understanding the concept of the chain of command. (Read about the Aaronic priesthood found in 1 Chronicles 24.) The head of the house is the husband, just as Christ is the head of the church (1 Tim. 3:4-5). We must recognize that God's plan of authority flows from a higher level to a lower level. We as Christians or secular leaders seem to sometimes forget this. (But sometimes it's easy to forget because there are no leaders in the leadership positions that can or will lead.) We can do ourselves a disservice by refusing to accept authority (Rom. 13:1). Let everyone be subject to God's governing authority. Jesus marveled at the Roman soldier's faith in (Luke 7:6-9) where he said I am also a man of authority. He told Jesus all He had to do was speak. To have authority we must have responsibility. We with authority are divinely ordained to use it responsibly. The paramount purpose of authority must be to be sensitive not only to the needs of those who serve but also to those being served.

One noted authority on management says: Authority may be more complex than realized by those in management. A person can and will accept communication as authoritative only when four conditions are met:

1. He can and does understand the communication.

2. At the time of his decision, he believes that it is compatible with his/her personal interests.

3. At the time of his decision, he believes that it is not inconsistent with the purpose of the organization.

4. He/She is able both mentally and physically to comply with it.

We are reminded not only of the complex nature of authority, but also of the attitudes of those reporting and receiving the information of the force at work in a leadership situation; the qualities of the leader, kind of followers, and those around must be identified.

Moses was leader of many, but he had to realize with the help of Jethro his father-in-law that if he did not appoint people under him to be leaders of smaller groups, that he would soon be no good to his people. So he had to delegate individuals to positions of leadership, forming a chain of command.

(Theodore Roosevelt once said, "The best executive has sense enough to pick the best people to do the work and restraint enough to stay out of their way and let them do their work.")

Moses was also concerned about being the right kind of leader for God's people. He was also concerned about a successor (someone to take his place) to lead the people into the Promised Land with the right direction.

Moses possessed outstanding leadership qualities that enabled him to succeed (Heb. 11:24, faith; v. 25, integrity; v. 26, vision; v. 27, decisiveness; v. 28, obedience; v. 29, responsibility). Moses is considered by most to be the greatest leader in the history of Israel. Christian leaders serve better when they are in the will of God. David recognized the fact that he was second under God as leader of His people.

He humbly attributed his rise to power to God. David constantly sought God's blessings; he knew the necessity of having God's blessings on his administrative team; today we need no less.

The study of Christian leadership would be incomplete unless the life of Christ is studied. Christ was leader by example. Christ makes it clear that true leadership is grounded in love, which is expressed by service. A leader must have obedience from his followers. They must be taught and trained, whether it be Christian or secular leadership. We must have clear-cut goals.

There must be sound committed men in leadership positions of Doth secular and Christian worlds. Leaders must motivate their followers with compassion and not just out of duty. There have been over the years many theories of motivational techniques. The primary motivator according to one theory is financial, but let us look a little further. Motivation can be decided as a process of stimulating an individual to take action that will lead to the fulfillment of a need or the accomplishment of a desired goal. If you have an intense craving to succeed, you will study and learn as much as you can in order to fulfill this ambition.

One has suggested that there are five basic needs which will motivate us: (1) survival, (2) safety, (3) a sense of belonging, (4) ego status, and (5) self-actualization.

Still another felt the upper-level motivators lead to behaviors, which are directly relevant to the work accomplished. While lower-level dissatisfiers promote behaviors that focus on issues to the work itself, he concluded that even when the lower-level needs are satisfied-and according to another are no longer sources of goal-directed behavior-there is still no reason to expect that individuals will perform any more effectively in their work. Why? Because the lower-level needs to serve primarily as maintenance factors; those needs that people assume for the most part will be adequately met. A good boss and good working conditions are examples of such needs. Few professional people would cite these as the job factors that motivate them most. Yet the minute either the boss or the working conditions become principle concerns, factors, like interesting job content and opportunity for advancement lose their power to motivate and the employer is in trouble. In short, effective job performance depends on the adequacy of both motivator and basic needs.

Motivational Factors

It's important for you to know what motivates you. Regardless of the circumstances on the job, there are still motivating factors that will cause you to continue working hard and doing a good job. I'm going to write down ten things that motivate us most, you decide in what order they affect you: (1) good pay, (2) chance for promotion, (3) respect for me as a person, (4) feeling my job is important, (5) opportunity for self-development and improvement, (6) large amounts of freedom on the job, (7) being told by my boss I do a good job, (8) opportunity to do interesting work, (9) getting a performance rating, and (10) steady employment.

Motivation is affected by age and personal circumstances and by the phase of life and career that you're going through at that moment. But that's not all. Motivation is affected by outside environment as well. For instance, at times of economic slumps, steady employment and good pay are both important; but when the economy is flourishing, people often take both job and pay for granted.

Factors that motivate us change at different stages of life (when we're first married, when we lose a job, when we near retirement, etc.). But there are many surprising similarities in how people rank the factors most important to them. "Respect for me as a person" is often no. 1. Also in general, steady employment as a motivating factor is more important in an economic slump.

One theory stresses that there are certain needs that are learned and socially acquired through interaction with the environment. This theory concerns three motives: the need to achieve, the need for power, the need for affiliation and how those needs affect the individual behavior in the workplace (environment). Each individual possesses these motives to varying degrees. Individuals who exhibit strong needs for achievement are particularly adaptable to work environment in which they can attain success through their own efforts, rather than by chance. The achievement motivation theory is largely a theory of entrepreneurship. Entrepreneurs seek out such environments.

People with strong achievement and power needs should be placed in an appropriate entrepreneurial or leadership work context. Their fundamental needs will motivate them efficiently.

Reinforcement theories assume that the consequences of a person's behavior determines his/her level of motivation. Behavior that is reinforced by a reward will be repeated; behaviors are learned as consequences occur in the form of rewards and punishments. To obtain desired results, it would depend on how the reinforcers are applied.

The expectancy theory of motivation allows for differences in individuals and holds that those individuals will be motivated by their personal expectation of rewards and their preferences for these rewards.

The equity theory holds that unfairness is a powerful motivating force in the workplace. It depends on comparison of perceived equity of pay and rewards among employees and comparison of compensation as related to factors such as education, experience, and seniority.

Leadership Theory

The gift of administration is very important for a leader; he must have the ability to administer and manage. Solomon was probably the greatest leader as for as administration is concerned. No one after him could control the same plan for their nation as Solomon. So eventually it split into southern kingdom of (Judah) and northern kingdom of (Israel)

Leadership is the process by which one individual influences others to accomplish desired goals. In the business of organization, the leadership process takes the form of a manager who influences subordinates to accomplish the goals defined by top management.

There could be two different kinds of leadership in an organization.

1. Formal Leaders. Those who are officially assigned leadership responsibilities within an organization.

2. Informal Leaders. Those who are not officially assigned leadership duties within the organization but may actually exercise the leadership duties. The two are not the same, yet both may exercise leadership behavior in influencing others.

   1. Formal Leader. Is someone officially invested with organizational

authority, power, and generally given the title of manager, executive, or supervisor. The amount of power is theoretically determined by the position occupied within the organization. Organizational promotion policies are designed to ensure that people with the necessary technical and leadership skills occupy the position of power.

2. Informal Leaders. Will not have a leadership title but will exercise a leadership function. The individual without formal authority, assignment of power, position, or even responsibility may by virtue-of a personal attitude or superior performance influence others and exercise leadership functions.

First, it is necessary to understand the nature of power within an organization, for effective use of individual power is the basis of leadership.

Six Variations of Individual Power in an Organizational Setting

1. Legitimate Power. This power is natural within the organizational structure. This power is assigned to an individual who occupies a specific position within that organization. Should the individual leave the position, the power stays with the position and does not follow the individual. This power is made legitimate within the organization as the individual is vested with the power. This assumption of power is generally signified by an official title, such as manager, vice president, director, supervisor, etc.

2. Reward Power. Also within the organizational structure in that managers are given administrative power over a range of rewards. Employees will be influenced by the possibility of receiving rewards for their work performance. These rewards can be very different and for a different reason, such as pay raises, promotional, managerial praises, statues, attention, etc. These rewards can be used to motivate workers, but if the manager cannot follow through with the reward potential, his/her power as a manager will be greatly reduced.

3. Coercive Power. This power is based on the manager's ability to discipline an employee. Discipline can be a range of options from a mild warning to dismissal. This action serves to discourage undesired behavior. We must remember that this will not promote desired employee performance and must be handled delicately. We must also

remember that a manager's ability to discipline workers may be union contracts or worker antidiscrimination laws. The manager must be sure the discipline taken against the employee does not exceed the offense of the employee.

4. Expert Power. This power comes from the experience of the manager, his/her individual skills, knowledge, abilities, or previous experience. Expert power comes from special knowledge or education. It is not related to age or job seniority since it often will depend upon educational achievements, not necessarily time on the job. This allows younger workers or people who are new to the workforce to gain recognition and influence within an organization. We must remember that expertise within an organization can change, depending on what is needed at the time.

5. Referent Power. This is power of one individual over another to influence by force of character or personal charisma. A manager who is particularly handsome, talented, or just plain likeable may be described by employees as inspiring and motivating. This person has charisma, and this will confer great power as a manager. This power can also come to us by the way we perceive others. In other words, we use total groups to arrive at the decisions we want by having everyone's input and cooperation.

6. Information Power. By possessing the knowledge of the marketplace and the means to move company products and critical information necessary for organizational functioning. This power is secured when access to the critical information is gained. Organizational power may be unrelated to the actual organizational position. A secretary, for instance, although low in rank may have a great deal of actual power since he/she has access to very important information. The genetic theory of leadership believes that leadership abilities are transmitted genetically. The phrase "Leaders are born, not made" sums up this approach.

Another theory of leadership can also be considered genetic because of the assumption that leaders are born, not made. Look at these personal traits necessary for leadership success.

1. Superior intelligence
2. Self-confidence

3. Effectiveness at communication
4. Decisiveness
5. Creativity

Have all been identified by various scientific researchers as characteristic traits of those who are successful in business?

Let's look at the following:

1. Superior intelligence: Learned

2. Self-confidence: Lots of work to be truly self-confident (build)

3. Effective communication: Learned experience by dealing with people of different personalities and background

4. Decisiveness: Learned experience to know when to and how to make decisions

5. Creativity: As we go through life every day, we learn to be creative.

No, my friend, leaders are not born, they are made. As I've said before, some of us have more qualities than others as far as being leaders, so we are more easily developed into leaders. Some who could be good leaders don't want to be, because they don't have the desire to accept the responsibility that goes with being a leader.

The minister is one who directs his flock and also serves (Luke 4:20). The word "minister" there means attendant (Acts 13:5). Paul, Apollo, and Cephas are considered ministers of Christ in Acts 26:26 and 1 Corinthians 4:1. In Acts 27:11, the helmsman had a great responsibility to guide the ship through the storms. The captain had to know it all. The helmsman was a very knowledgeable seaman who followed orders. He was second in command. So the minister is considered the helmsman who is in charge of directing His church through the storm, hardships, conflicts, etc., that come his way; he must be able to handle it. The minister must have the right understanding to be able to direct others to the right course.

It is well for us to bear in mind the importance of singling out those who display administrative and leadership qualities-whether they be practicing those gifts in or out of the traditional church-and do all we can to enhance and encourage their development, so the lives of many will be blessed and fulfilled. Christians will be more useful than ever, and their influence in this growing evil world will be more effective. We need this force in our community and in our world, because of the continual growing violence such as drive-by shootings that are taking the lives of the innocent. We must have some kind of direction to control this violence, not by force but by creative leadership.

According to over two hundred managers in a survey for American Managers Association, they all agreed that the single most important skill of an executive is their ability to get along with people. This ability is rated more vital than intelligence, decisiveness, knowledge, or job skills. By definition, style is the way a leader carrier out their function, how they are perceived by those they attempt to lead. The more we adapt our style of leadership behavior to meet the particular needs of our followers, the more effective we become in meeting our goals.

We must decide which leadership styles are most effective in different situations. Successful leaders adapt their leadership behavior to meet the needs of the group and the particular situations. There are many ways to exercise leadership, whether in academics, military, religion, economics, politics, or society. Events throughout history have made great men, and great men have made great events happen. We must always be positive in our efforts to lead in any situation. Mood and conditions often describe the kind of leaders who emerge to meet the challenge, whether it be government, business, or our churches. The pressures of life have dictated the success of men like Billy Graham, who always emphasizes God's interest in the individual, bringing meaning and purpose to people who are searching for their niche in life.

The effective leader must always consider present conditions. He must be alert to the needs of the group now and have the best method of getting results. A leader must be able to keep in step with the times and make the best of every situation. The Christian leader cannot be driven by the thirst for power. He must always consider the need of his followers before his own.

A leader with flexibility is able to clarify and suggest the best course of action at any time. Today, we must have leaders that are creative and innovative enough to keep up with the times. The leader must know their group capabilities, analyze the situation, and be able to delegate responsibility and authority.

We must be able to distinguish between management and leadership. Management is a specialty of leadership in which the goals of the organization is a must to meet. Leadership involves working with and through people to accomplish goals. These can be any goals personal or business.

The Democratic Concept; Government Leaders

We the people elect representatives to represent us in the white house. They are supposed to carry out our wants and needs of policies. Our elected officials are there to assist, suggest, and allow adequate communication to flow so the group is alerted of the problems, and then they can be resolved. This is just one example of a leadership style; there are others. The ideal blend of an individual is to develop their own natural gifts and develop their own leadership traits through diligent work in the area of Christian or secular leadership. What about spiritual abilities? If a person has leadership abilities, does this require special training? Leadership qualities cannot be explained solely on the grounds of natural ability. Were there people in the Bible and secular world who were gifted leaders, that because God touched their life in a special way? Possibly! We see people in the political arena and in the complex business world go to the top because they manifest a strong, forceful personality. This drive may cause us to think they are natural leaders. Natural leaders are usually thought of as born leaders, yet he leads only because of circumstances. He came on the scene when leadership was needed, when there was a fire to put out. In this area, we usually think of the Napoleons, Hitlers, the dictators, or the dominant personalities who have shown some characteristics of leadership. But this kind of leadership is often weak.

He can only impose his powers of authority over others through a strong will. The tyrant-type leader is found not only in the political world, but also in most other areas of life. A good leader must work from a group situation so as to have creative thinking and continue to move forward and provide change for the group.

The tyrant leader's followers will not be permanent. It will be a sacrificial loyalty that lasts for a short time. To be a solid and effective leader, he must consider the desires of his followers. We must learn as leaders to develop the talent and gifts God has given us and not try to imitate others, because we will end up discouraged and disappointed. Can we train leaders? As we look back, it has always been assumed for centuries that leadership was inherited or passed from generation to generation, that leaders were born not made. (I believe the only sure way to have effective leaders is to train them.) It was later realized that leaders could be trained and developed. We began to focus on a person's personality and skills, which might be waiting to be developed. Heads of all groups must believe in training their leaders. It must be of necessity. The best leaders in the Bible were trained and developed for their position of leadership, even though they felt called by God to lead in certain areas of Christian work. So should leaders be trained accordingly in the secular world of industry. Samuel was set up to train the prophets in the Old Testament (1 Sam. 19:18-20); there were many prophets trained in schools set up in those days for that purpose. The theological training centers or seminaries of today are a result of those Old Testament training centers. These training centers were set up to develop, train, and educate men in the area of leadership functions necessary to do God's work.

So we can safely say spiritual gifts can be developed. We must realize that our young people, whether they be in the Christian world or in the secular world, must be trained, taught, and developed in the area of leadership (the same way athletes are trained), as much as possible throughout their life because someday they will be our leaders. We need strong, developed leaders, not only in the Christian world, but also in the political and secular worlds as well.

An Approach to Basic Leadership Training

1. A Plan to Develop Potential Leaders
   Every firm must continually give thoughts to training others in their organization for positions of authority. There must be training to provide constant innovation and motivation into the organization's successful direction and guidance that employees need. This helps to destroy negativism and encourages personal initiative. Otherwise, the organization will grow stagnant.

2. An Inventory of Positions
   The best people in any organization should be placed in varies areas of responsibilities. This requires study of personnel (an inventory of people); the organization can then find the right person for each function and then train them accordingly. If the position is not there, the man should not be put there. We must set up the parameters of the job. An important task of management and leadership should be to prepare job descriptions so that each participant understands his/her respective roles and duties.

3. An Inventory of Potential Leaders
   There should always be a search for potential leaders in any organization. This is done by personal contact and interviews. We must consider all the following plus factors: skill, personality, intelligence, motivation, values, judgments, and character. These are just a few of the requirements to be considered.

Interviews

Sensitivity. The ability to see what others can't. The capacity to stretch powers.

Flexibility. The ability to adjust quickly. A willingness to abandon old ways and to move past obvious boundaries of problems. The courage to establish norms. The ability to break down problems and find solutions to solve them.

Leadership is too often considered a product of one's natural abilities and personality traits, including mental enthusiasm and power to persuade. These qualities can go a long way in leading people. The main quality is the willingness to sacrifice for the sake of the determined objectives. We keep referring back to Christian leadership because of the example-spiritual leaders are willing to sacrifice themselves which makes them good leaders. A Christian leader blends both spiritual and natural qualities together to influence others not only by his own power and personality, but also by the power of the Holy Spirit.

The Spirit of God can enhance the leadership potential of spiritual men. This book is written to benefit both Christian organizations and the secular business world of industry and politics. It is my hope that it will benefit all who read it. When leadership is defined, it is frequently attempted to set it in terms of style. In doing this, a leader is described as to how he operates, rather than who he is.

So we tend to characterize the leader by our own perceptions of his style. The human skills are of primaly importance today. One has said, "I will pay more for the ability to deal with people than any otller ability under the sun."

Studies have shown that most people prefer a developmental, people-oriented supervisor regardless of their own styles they themselves practice.

While a concern for relationship is represented by democratic leaders' behavior, this has been common because it is thought that a leader influences his followers in one of two ways:

1. He tells them what and how to do things (authoritarian style).
2. He can involve them in the solutions of the task (Democratic style). It has been said this way: Tell me and I'll forget. Show me and I'll remember. Involve me and I'll understand.

The authoritarian leader is thought to have grown up in a home where he was constantly put down by a strong authority figure. He has not only been given the opportunity to express himself, without parental guidance and words of encouragement and compliments for accomplishments, he never learned to feel good about himself. This comes out in adult life without us even realizing it.

There is a big difference in leading and commanding. In hiring people, we should look for people who are looking for careers and relationships with a firm and us with them. Commanders are like directors who put the organization above its people.

The Leaders

Guides and develops the individual so they can better shape their destiny. The true leader does not get his people to work by intimidation; he does it by motivation and keeping morale high. The same style of leadership cannot be used in every situation. Both leaders and followers are different.

So each situation requires a leader who can adapt to the problem, analyze it, and direct his followers to solve it. Both leader and organization should be able to modify their style of leadership to cope with the constant and continuous changes that take place from time to time. We must be mature enough in our leadership style to be flexible. We must be flexible in the application of our style. There is no single personality that is effective in leaders; they vary widely in their temperament and abilities. But there must be action from all types.

There must be loyalty from both sides. A leader must be able to give proper support by showing continuous enthusiasm and assurance. He must always be a source of encouragement to his followers. All types of leaders must have confidence in themselves and the ability to direct their group to complete their goals. Faith is a very important asset (Heb. 11:1). Faith is the substance of things hoped for, the evidence of things not seen. This-says things are already there so you see how vital faith is in a leadership position. You must have faith first of all in yourself, second in people. When a leader believes this, he will be able to discover human desires. For us to motivate others, we must have a larger view of ourselves. This gives us a better sense of value. Leadership is sometimes a lonely position.

We may feel at times that we are ignored and even betrayed by those we felt we could count on in a bind. Strong faith and confidence in one's knowledge and abilities are vital. They provide a balance in time of trouble when you must stand against all odds: We can only see ourselves as others see us, so as leaders we must realize this and use it in our makeup. The leader may be temperamental if he is under stress. We cannot go to the office party tonight and take the same type of atmosphere into the office the next day. Emotional stability is one of the most important processions for effective leadership. Everyone experiences tension, frustrations, and conflict with others. A mark of maturity is having the ability to handle these kinds of conflicts. This will determine how successful you are.

We as leaders must understand that our emotional stability is indicated in how we deal with people. When we can stop condemning people in our minds for their mistakes, we will develop a better self-image. Try treating others as if they have value.

Attitudes, Styles, and Personality

The most important traits needed by leaders are the following: an understanding of human nature, sociableness, intelligence, dependability, loyalty, friendliness, and faithfulness. He must be a creative and innovative thinker and a person of action. A good leader must have the ability to look beyond self and see the traits of others that will help the organization. The personality of a leader plays a vital role in the installation of change. Once he is there, there will be no change or movement without him. The iron will, vision, and daring of an exceptional leader are needed to mobilize existing attitudes into the drive of change. A leader must have a good and healthy ego; otherwise, he cannot kindle the desire in others. The best leaders are people who know themselves. Self-improvement courses can help to improve one's personality and give him confidence. We must all be aware of our state of mind especially people in leadership positions. Leaders must have the self-realization of power, which motivated them to achieve beyond the average level. This helps us as leaders to meet our objectives. As we become familiar with our own needs, we begin to understand others. One's self-image is essential for us to develop in the area of leadership. For overall effectiveness, we must develop our attitudes, styles, and personality to become respected and outstanding leaders.

There is always a price for leadership. It always costs. Leaders must be committed, reassuring, and emotionally stable. To become a good leader, we must be persistent. We must continually do research to keep up with the changing procedures and times; it is a constant effort to be the best we can be.

Criticism should always make us better, because when we are criticized we know where our shortcomings are and can improve upon them. Because if we are not told how we come across to people, how do we improve? Leaders must realize that it is a lonely position at the top sometimes. We must realize that there are times when we must be away from the crowd, alone by ourselves. We must take time to think because the objective requires us to do this. Even though leadership can be a lonely position, it is up to us not to let it be, because whether we admit it or not, we need people; we need their emotional support.

To be an effective leader, we cannot run too far ahead of our followers. So for the leader to identify with his people, he must take the time to know them. He must share in their victories, defeats, and emotions. The tough decision comes for a leader when he has the unpleasant task of removing someone because of lack of performance. But these kinds of decisions have to be made because it affects the performances of the group as a whole.

There must always be healthy competition because without it, the leader and the organization will surely fail. Because this is what makes our free enterprise system work. Each of us should know who we are and be the best we can be and in what we do. But we should not so prideful in ourselves that the other person does not count. But we should be proud of our accomplishments. Besides the leader must be able to appoint people to the group he leads, which after all should be a group effort. A leader should be respected in order for him to get the job done. But we as leaders should not get to the point where we feel like we are indispensable. Our most important commodity is time. We learn how to effectively train ourselves to use our time to its best advantage. We must be able to accept criticism and rejection and be willing to pay the price of success.

There are far too many people today willing to settle for mediocrity in leadership qualities, whether it be in the Christian, secular, business, industrial, or in the political world.

No one cares what office or title you've held in the past but only the character of your heart and mind at present. Mediocrity cannot be a part of a leader; he must require from his followers people who are committed to high efficiency and quality. We should not be concerned with better programs to build quality but look to our followers to produce better quality.

The encouragement provided for moving up the ladder is competence. It is competence that gives an individual his promotions and raises. Competence separates the good leader from the mediocre leader. Competence should be the one quality that is most notable in a leader. Any time you go to make changes in an organization you best do it with competence and confidence, along with all the facts pertaining to the changes to be made. A competent leader is also able to see flaws in the workmanship and proposals to anticipate problems before they arise. In any situation, a leader must show competence and confidence, and he must be in control at all times. There has to be someone in the area of leadership to guide, direct, and make it work. There can be no substitute for competent leadership. Competent top leadership is more than just reading a book; we must take continual action for improvement. For priorities to become a reality, we must establish the proper use of time, for without it we will not see proper results. We must have clearly defined goals and a desire to achieve them. The leader with goals that are clearly defined will accomplish much more than the leader without them.

The more competent you are, the more confidence the other fellow will have in you to accomplish the task. If you have position as well as the authority, there is no question as to who you are. It is easier to get people to respond to you if you have a pleasant personality. Character is a very important part of your makeup; it tells people who you are, your integrity, ethics, honesty, reliability, personal morals and sincerity. If a person knows your character, you will get a much better response from them. Your character is measured by the willingness of putting yourself on the line to maintain honesty and dependability. There will be dynamic result found in leadership where a person will make those sacrifices to continually strengthen and improve himself.

Leadership development is like success, it is a never-ending process through the never-ending training and development of abilities. One must realize that there are times when his attitude and ambitions will need to be modified. Like anything else in life, we must continually search out people with leadership abilities. It is vital to the success of any group or organization. The person we select for leadership positions must have a positive attitude and character, and a good personality is important. We should first assign duties that are not too critical, and as they develop,
responsibility can be increased. If they can follow through, they will show potential as well as ability to take action when a decision is called for. A self-starting individual shows leadership potential because this shows motivation; he can understand the situation and be able to select the best course of action.

Important: Some Suggestions Would Be as Follows

1. He must be able to carry out assignments.

2. Must be able to reach group goals and be compatible with others in the group.

3. Must be organized. Be able to take and give orders. Be responsible.

4. Be able to show others what and how to do things.

I say again training our leaders is very important once a selection has been made. A person with competence, confidence and is accepted and well respected must be in control of the plan. A person must be screened when he/she is selected for leadership, must be emotionally stable, must have perseverance, his/her attitude must be right, and with an even temperament is helpful. A potential leader is continually trained and supervised by his superiors during a period of time such as an apprentice would be. The trainer must always be available to the trainee for direction and advice. They should offer criticism with much tact, so as not to alert the trainee of his shortcomings.

Tell-tale signs of the training being effective would be the following: quality and volume of work done, stability of his/her group, the number of complaints from the followers and leaders of the group. In other words, the performance, quality, and cohesiveness of the group of both leader and follower.

Motivation is the primary function of a leader. To be a strong and effective leader, there must be proper motivation. No matter what style of leadership you use, the key to getting people to follow is motivation. We should never belittle or criticize our followers in the presence of others. We should never play favorites or not have the time when our followers need us. We should be able to make decisions quickly. We should always let our followers know that we are conscious of their needs as a group and also as individuals. To show your followers you are concerned and care about them as a person, that in itself is motivation. Another way to motivate your followers is to allow them the opportunity to participate in the decision-making solutions directly related to the task.

I think Christian organizations lack in the area of motivation because they assume motivation is always there. Dedication to the Lord is very important to help motivate people. It is not to replace it. I think if we fail to use the principals of motivation, we are depriving our Christian organizations of a very valuable resource. A leader that can show his/her people that they have the ability to help them satisfy their wants and needs, they will follow them willingly and enthusiastically.

Promotions

We must be very careful when it comes to promoting people, that we don't promote them beyond their abilities to a "level of incompetence." There are people who can function at any level, and there are others who can't go beyond a certain level, or it would be total disaster. We cannot go beyond our abilities.

We as managers and department heads are in the business of getting things done with and through people. We must realize what a workable style would be to get the goals accomplished in a given situation. So again, I say a manager must be competent and qualified to handle the task in front of him.

We must realize that as managers and leaders in planning our goals and objectives. We must be able to bring together the resources to meet our goals and objectives such as people, capital, and equipment to accomplish our task in the most effective way. This would include our goals that are short term, midterm, and long term. We must always be able to meet our goals within a certain time frame. We must have goal setting to accomplish our objectives; without them there would be too much wasted time. We must have goals and plans on how to reach our final objectives. Our goals should not only be specific, but must also be attainable. Specific objectives could be stating the objective, reasons for achieving the objective, outline to achieve the objectives.

Timing; Assistance; Cost

There must be specific objectives made by leaders to be able to accomplish their goals. The planning process is very involved; without it there can be no progress. Planning takes time both in personal and business spheres. We should start our plans as far in advance as we possibly can. Because of the involvement of all aspects, procedures, dates, and objectives to be accomplished.

For the Christian group, just because they were taught in Sunday school that Jesus was coming soon, they neglect the planning and results. However true this is, it should not hinder the planning and growth of Christian leaders to be qualified to meet their goals. We must each know what our jobs are, and this comes from planning.

Organizational planning is at the forefront of all planning, because it clarifies the lines of responsibility.

Establishing a meaningful purpose for our goals, such as establishing relationships, setting up training procedures, which is one of the most important ingredients, and understanding what committed leadership is before starting a successful training program. We will attempt to explain the above. If you can grasp the last few pages to the point where you put them into a plan and organize them correctly, they will benefit your organization.

Planning and Organization

Are essential but alone they are insufficient for desired results in leadership. To accomplish common goals of an organization involves planning and organizing.

1. Selection of people
2. Communication
3. Delegation
4. Firm decision making

Selection of personnel is very crucial because if the wrong people are hired, it is highly unlikely the organization will survive. But bear in mind that qualified people are not always available. This means that if our prospect has some of the qualifications, we must be prepared to train and develop them in other areas. We must have the time to think the position through and be able to pick the most qualified people or at least the people with the most potential. Before we go outside the organization, we should look for people within our own ranks to be promoted if the potential is there. Whether we hire from within our own ranks or outside, the employee must continually be evaluated for performance.

Transfer of Work/Authority, Acceptance of Responsibility, and the Importance of Follow-up

We cannot stress the fact enough that for a leader to be in the position he holds, he must be qualified to direct the people that are promoted and hired. This is why continual training is, needed. His task is to bring all ingredients together so as to achieve the common goals. In this area, communication is one of the most important ingredients in getting the task accomplished. Part of communication is being able to listen and knowing when to listen. We must plan our communication carefully; not only that, but we must plan what we will say. The starting point of communication is human needs. Just as leadership should be continual training, so should communication. Speaking and listening are two very important ingredients. One way of indicating how important delegation is, is this statement: "A man's value to his organization is not measured by what he has on his desk, but by what passes over it." This goes to show how important it is to delegate. When a leader cannot delegate, he will constantly be involved in secondary details that will keep him away from his primary responsibilities. When leaders delegate, more can be accomplished better and faster. Delegation carries with it some important basic ideas: transfer of work/authority, acceptance of responsibility, the importance of follow-up.

Work to Be Delegated

Minor decisions should be delegated so the leader can go on to more important functions. When a leader has a subordinate who is more qualified in that area, especially when it is a specialized shop, he must delegate to give himself more time to increase his overall competence. Disciplinary matters should never be delegated because the final decision will be the leaders anyway.

Delegation should be given to those who seek additional responsibility and to those who show potential leadership in the future, and the leader will be able to evaluate their performance in a more positive light.

The person in whom the delegated responsibility is given should be trustworthy, confident, and accountable for his/her actions. Authority should be given so the job can be performed correctly; he should have the freedom to perform the delegated task. There should be adequate feedback or results of the project. Regular feedback will give us a sense of progress and accomplish.

Rules of Delegation

1. Don't wait until you have too much work to delegate.

2. Don't be reluctant to delegate, but have the patience to wait for its completion.

3. If it takes longer than usual, there may be some question as to the leaders, judgment, of the correct person to delegate to.

The person doing the initiating of delegating should be an effective communicator. The relationship between the supervisor and subordinate should be sound for the delegation process to work properly. For a supervisor to function well on his/her job, they must have relaxation outside the job. Delegation can help in this area.

There must be good decision making. This is a major quality for effective leadership. The leader must be able to think and act on their feet. The leader must have good timing and must have the ability to reason, the power of observation, and the correct attitude toward people. He must be positive and logical in his/her decision along with planning, organizing, and directing.

There Is Also Controlling

Planning and organizing goals need to be approved. They must meet the conditions set forth, for results to be achieved. The experienced leader continually uses his mistakes for improving future results. The experienced leader does things in order; in other words, he has a system of both his private and professional life. Because of his/her experience, he has a better sense of timing and also knows where to find helpful information. All these qualities come from experience and training. These steps are characteristic of a seasoned and experienced leader who can control the situation after the other operations have been put in place.

Another Ingredient Is Time Management

Experienced leaders know how to calculate their time because of their know-how. By combining knowledge, experience, and thinking, they can perform the job without hesitation. For as professionals, we must continue to question and question about each particular job, even though we think we know it well. We must at all times remain in control under pressure, we must know people who we are dealing with for proper timing to work.

We must know by and through human nature what people are capable of under similar circumstances.

All too often when a new leader or manager takes over a vacated position, he will have to make changes. For instance, if the old leader was lax in enforcing breaks and lunches from being too long, the new leader needs to be sure his/her timing is right when instituting changes to keep these areas under control. However, it is human nature to resist change; we can see that correct timing is of vital importance when promoting change. So we must use logic and analysis for every situation that we want to change. This must be done for the benefit of the leader and the organization. Information is a very important item when it comes to timing. Without proper information, there can be no decision made to go forward. So good up-to-date information is vital.

The four managerial tasks we have considered here are vital to the success of any good leader. Regardless of the leadership style, these four responsibilities cannot be limited. Planning, organizing, directions, and controlling are four vital ingredients of any successful leader. But to accomplish all these takes both technical and human skills.

Guidance

A leader must be confident in himself before he can convince anyone to have confidence in him. So some important ingredients for a leader are confidence, honesty, integrity, and we as leaders above all must be competent to handle each situation.

As we move up the ladder, there are critical factors to contend with. People both inside and outside our organization will see the type of leader we are.

Above all, we must have honest integrity in all our dealings, whether it be as a leader or in our own private life. We must not forget that we all interpret things differently, and what might seem honest and aboveboard to us might not look that way to our people and others outside our organization. The leader cannot afford to offend people's morals if he expects loyalty. So integrity must become evident when a person displays consistency in character and conduct. To acquire these qualities takes time and continual feedback from both our people and outsiders. Leadership is like success-it is a never-ending process.

Leaders must be able to look ahead to the future. They must continually motivate, train, and guide their people so they can achieve their future goals. They must be involved in the operations and decision-making process.

There are always difficult situations a leader has to take care of both of their own personnel and the people above them. These situations require tactful solutions. A tactful person can bring two opposing viewpoints together without comprising his own principals. I feel that 95 percent of our problems as leaders are personal problems. Where people are involved, there are always conflicts that require tactful solutions.

We as leaders must be able to choose between being liked and being respected. We all want to be liked, and we don't necessarily have to be liked to be respected. Some leaders are not liked as individuals but are respected for their leadership abilities and competence at getting things done. When respect is lost, it is very difficult to regain. It doesn't matter whether it is an organization or an individual. To regain respect after it is lost it is an uphill battle.

The marks of a good leader, whether it is Christian, secular, business, or political, are those that demand the very best from their people. We as leaders cannot allow our competitors to have the best products on the market. We must always strive to be the best at what we do. We cannot allow our products to be inferior to our competitors. We must set goals to be able to achieve our objective one step at a time. To achieve excellence, our goals must be continually pursued.

One of the most important areas to be able to reach our goals of excellence must be discipline. To have discipline means we have conquered ourselves. To manage ourselves means setting proper priorities in a way to where the most will be accomplished, for we must always give top performance in every task we undertake to do.

As leaders we must continually pressing forward-researching, studying, motivating, guiding, directing. Striving in every area to be the best at what we do and always with honest integrity as the top priority on our list.

We must always remember that success is a journey, not a destination. Because success is not finished until you are.

These are my own personal views, combined with the knowledge I've gathered from other writers. This book is written hopefully to awake-the desire in others to become good leaders in their communities, whether Christian, business, and political, to get serious about leadership and help develop any gleam of potential in this area. I thank you for the time spent in this book and hope it will benefit you as much as it has me.

New Testament Scripture References from NKJV
Religious Leaders from New Testament

Mark 3:14:	Then He appointed twelve, that they might be-with Him and that He might send them out to preach.
Acts 2:42:	And they continued steadfastly in the apostles' doctrine and fellowship, in the breaking of bread, and in prayers.
Acts 5:12:	And through the hands of the apostles many signs and wonders were done among the people. And they were all of one accord in Solomon's porch.
2 Corinthians 12:12:	Truly the signs of an apostle were accomplished among you with all perseverance, in signs and wonders and mighty deeds.
Acts 4:37:	having land sold it, and brought the money and laid it at the Apostles feet.

Acts 6:1-6

V. 1: now in those days, when the number of disciples were multiplying, there arose a complaint against the Hebrews by the Hellenists, because their widows were neglected in the daily distribution.

V. 2: Then the twelve summoned the multitude of disciples and said, "It is not desirable that we should leave the word of God and serve tables.

V. 3: Therefore, brethren, seek out from among you seven men of good reputation, full of the Holy Spirit and Wisdom, whom we may appoint over this business.

V. 4: but we will give ourselves continually to prayer and to the ministry of the word."

V. 5: And the saying pleased the whole multitude. And they chose Stephen, a man full of faith and the Holy Spirit, and Philip Prochorus, Nicanor, Timon, Parmenas, and Nicolas, a proselyte from Antioch,

V. 6: Whom they set before the apostles; and when they had prayed, they laid hands on them.

Acts 5:1-11

V. 1: But a certain man named Ananias, with Saphira his wife, sold a possession.

V. 2: And he kept back part of the proceeds, his wife also being aware of it, and brought a certain part and laid it at the apostles' feet.

V. 3: But Peter said, ''Ananias, why has Satan filled your heart to lie to the Holy Spirit and keep back part of the price of the land for yourself?

V. 4: While it remained, was it not your own? And after it was sold, was it not in your own control? Why have you conceived this thing in your heart? You have not lied to men but to God."

V. 5: Then Ananias, hearing these words, fell down and breathed his last. So great fear came upon all those who heard these things.

V. 6: And the young men arose and wrapped him up, carried him out and buried him.

V. 7: Now it was about three hours later when his wife came in, not knowing what had happened.

V. 8: And Peter answered her, "Tell me whether you sold the land for so much?" She said, "Yes, for so much."

V. 9: Then Peter said to her, "How is it that you have agreed together to test the Spirit of the Lord? Look, the feet of those who have buried your husband are at the door, and they will carry you out."

V. 10: Then immediately she fell down at his feet and breathed her last. And the young men came and found her dead, and carrying her out, buried her by her husband.

V. 11: So great fear came upon the church and on all who heard these things.

Acts 8:14: Now when the apostles who were at Jerusalem heard that Samaria had received the word of God, they sent Peter and John to them.

Acts 9:32: Now it came to pass, as Peter went through all parts of the country, that he also came down to the saints who dwelt in Lydda.

Galatians 1:19: But, I saw none of the other apostles except James the Lord's brother.

Acts 1:21-22
V. 21: "Therefore, of these men who have accompanied us all the time that the Lord Jesus went in and out among us.
V. 22: beginning from the baptism of John to that day when He was taken up from us, one of these must become a witness with us of His resurrection."

Acts 12:2: Then he killed James the brother of John with the sword.

Acts 20:28: Therefore take heed to yourselves and to all the flock, among which the Holy Spirit has made you overseers, to shepherd the church of God which He purchased with His own blood.

Acts 11:30: This they also did, and sent it to the elders by the hands of Barnabas and Saul.

Acts 15:2, 4, 6, 22, 23
V. 2: Therefore, when Paul and Barnabas had no small dissension and dispute with them, they determined that Paul and Barnabas and certain others of them should go up to Jerusalem, to the apostles and elders, about this question.
V. 4: And when they had come to Jerusalem, they were received by the church and the Apostles and the elders; and they reported all things that God had done with them.

V. 6: Now the apostles and elders came together to consider this matter.
V. 22: Then it pleased the apostles and elders, with the whole church, to send chosen men of their own company to Antioch with Paul and Barnabas, Namely, Judas who was also named Barnabas, and Silas, Leading men among the brethren.
V. 23: They wrote this letter by them: The apostles, the elders, and the brethren, to the brethren who are of the Gentiles in Antioch, Syria, and Cilicia: GREETINGS.

Acts 14:23: So when they had appointed elders in every church, and prayed with fasting, they commended them to the Lord in whom they had believed.

Titus 1:5-9
V. 5: For the reason I left you in Crete, that you should set in order the things that are lacking, and appoint elders in every city that I commanded you.
V. 6: If a man is blameless, the husband of one wife, having faithful children not accused of dissipation and insubordination.
V. 7: For a bishop must be blameless, as a steward of God, not self-willed, not quick-tempered, not given to wine, not violent, not greedy for money,
V. 8: but hospitable, a lover of what is good, sober-minded, just, holy, self-controlled,
V. 9: holding fast the faithful word as he has been taught, that he may be able, by sound doctrine; both to exhort and convict those who contradict.

1 Timothy 3:1: This is a faithful saying: If a man desires the position of a bishop, he desires a good work.

Philippians 1:1: Paul and Timothy, bondservants of Jesus Christ, to all the saints in Christ Jesus who are in Philippi, with the bishops and deacons.

Read 1 Timothy 3

1 Corinthians 12:28: And God has appointed these in the church: first Apostles, second Prophets, third teachers, after that miracles, then gifts of healings, helps, administrations,

	varieties of tongues.
Acts 6:2:	Then the twelve summoned the multitude of the disciples and said, "It is not desirable that we should leave the word of God and serve tables.
Romans 16:1:	I commend to you Phoebe our sister, who is a servant of the church in Cenchrea.

Charismatic Leaders
New Testament Scripture References

1 Corinthians 12:28-31
V. 28: And God has appointed these in the church: first apostles, second prophets, third teachers, after that miracles, then gifts of healings, helps, administrations, varieties of tongues.
V. 29: Are all apostles? Are all prophets? Are all teachers? Are all workers of miracles?
V. 30: Do all have gifts of healings? Do all speak with tongues? Do all interpret?
V. 31: But earnestly desire the best gifts. And yet I show you a more excellent way.

Ephesians 4:11:	And He Himself gave some to be apostles, some prophets, some evangelists, and some pastors and teachers.

1 Corinthians 14: 29-32
V. 29: Let two or three prophets speak, and let the others judge.

V. 30: But if anything is revealed to another who sits by, let the first keep silent.
V. 31: For you can all prophesy one by one, that all may learn and all may be encouraged.
V. 32: And the spirits of the prophets are subject to the prophets.

Theological Dimensions of Leadership in the Bible

Romans 13:1: Let every soul be subject to the governing authorities. For there is no authority except from God, and the authorities that exist are appointed by God.

Daniel 4:32: And they shall drive you from men, and your dwelling shall be with the beast of the field. They shall make you eat grass like oxen; and seven times shall pass over you, until you know that the most high rules in the kingdom of men, and gives it to whomever He chooses.

Daniel 5:21: Then He was driven from the sons of men, his heart was made like the beasts, and his dwelling was with the wild donkeys. They fed him with grass like an oxen, and his body was wet with the dew of heaven, till he knew that the Most High God rules in the kingdom of men, and appoints over it whomever He chooses.

Exodus 4
V. 1: Then Moses answered and said, "But suppose they will not believe me or listen to my voice; suppose they say, "The Lord has not appeared to you."
V. 2: So the Lord said to him, "What is that in your hand?" He said, "A rod."
V. 3: And He said, "Cast it on the ground." So he cast it on the ground, and it became a serpent; and Moses fled from it.
V. 4: Then the Lord said to Moses, "Reach our your hand and take it by the tail" (and he reached out his hand and caught it, and it became a rod in his hand),
V. 5: that they might believe that the Lord God of their fathers, the God of Abraham, the God of Isaac, and the God of Jacob, has appeared to you.
V. 6: Furthermore the Lord said to him, "Now put your hand in your bosom." And he put his hand in his bosom, and when he took it out, behold his hand was leprous, like snow.
V. 7: And He said, "Put your hand in your bosom again." So he put his hand in his bosom again, and drew it out of his bosom, and behold,

and behold it was restored like his other flesh.

V. 8: "Then it will be, if they do not believe you, nor heed the message of the first sign, that they may believe the message of the latter sign.

V. 9: And it shall be, if they do not believe even these two signs, or listen to your voice, that you shall take water from the river and pour it on dry land. The water which you take from the river will become blood on the dry land.

V. 10: Then Moses said to the Lord, "O my Lord, I am not eloquent, neither before or since You have spoken to Your servant; but I am slow of speech and slow of tongue."

V. 11: So the Lord said to him, "Who has made man's mouth? Or who makes the mute, the deaf, the seeing or the blind? Have not I, the Lord?

V. 12: Now therefore, go, and I will be with your mouth and teach you what you shall say."

V. 13: But he said, "O my Lord, please send by the hand of whomever else you may send."

V. 14: So the anger of the Lord was kindled against Moses, and He said, "Is not Aaron the Levite your brother? I know that he can speak well. And look, he is also coming out to meet you. When he sees you, he will be glad in his heart.

V. 15: Now you shall speak to him and put the words in his mouth. And I will be with your mouth and with his mouth, and I will teach you what you shall do.

V. 16: So he shall be your spokesman to the people. And he himself shall be as a mouth for you, and you shall be to him as God.

V. 17: And you shall take this rod in your hand, with which you shall do the signs."

V. 18: So Moses went and returned to Jethro his father-in-law, and said to him, "Please let me go and return to my brethren who are in Egypt, and see whether they are still alive." And Jethro said to Moses, "Go in peace."

V. 19: Now the Lord said to Moses in Midian, "Go, return to Egypt; for all the men who sought your life are dead."

V. 20: Then Moses took his wife and his sons and set out on a donkey, and he returned to the land of Egypt. And Moses took the rod of God in his hand.

V. 21: And the Lord said to Moses, "When you go back to Egypt, see that you do all those wonders before Pharaoh which I have put in your hand. But I will harden his heart, so that he will not let the people

V. 22: Then you shall say to Pharaoh, "Thus says the Lord: 'Israel is My son, My firstborn.
V. 23: So I say to you, let My son go so that he may serve Me. But if you refuse to let him go, indeed I will kill your son, your firstborn.'"
V. 24: And it came to pass on the way, at the encampment, that the Lord met him and sought to kill him.
V. 25: Then Zipporah took a sharp stone and cut off the foreskin of her son and cast it at Moses' feet, and said, "Surely you are a husband of blood to me?"
V. 26: So he let him go. Then she said, "You are a husband of blood!"- Because of the circumcision.
V. 27: And the Lord said to Aaron, "Go into the wilderness to meet Moses." So he went and met him on the mountain of God, and kissed him.
V. 28: So Moses told Aaron all the words of the Lord who had sent him, and all the signs which He had commanded him.
V. 29: Then Moses and Aaron went and gather together all the elders of the children of Israel.
V. 30: And Aaron spoke all the words which the Lord had spoken to Moses. Then he did the signs in the sight of the people.
V. 31: So the people believed; and when they had heard that the Lord had visited the children of Israel and that he had looked on their affliction, then they bowed their heads and worshipped.

Joshua 1
V. 1: After the death of Moses the servant of the Lord, it came to pass that the Lord spoke to Joshua the son of Nun, Moses, assistant saying:
V. 2: Moses My servant is dead. Now therefore, arise, go over this Jordan, you and all this people, to the land which I am giving to them-the children of Israel.
V. 3: Every place that the sole of your foot will tread upon I have given you, as I said to Moses.
V. 4: From the wilderness and this Lebanon as far as the great river, the river Euphrates, all the land of the Hittites, and the great sea toward the going down of the sun, shall be your territory.
V. 5: No man shall be able to stand before you all the days of your life; as I was with Moses, so I will be with you. I will not leave you nor forsake you.
V. 6: Be strong and of good courage, for to this people you shall divide as an inheritance the land which I swore to their fathers to give them.

V. 7: Only be strong and very courageous, that you may observe to do according to the law which Moses My servant commanded you; do not turn from it to the right hand or to the left, that you may prosper where you go.

V. 8: This book of the law shall not depart from your mouth, but you shall meditate in it day and night, that you observe to according to all that is written in it. For then you will make your way prosperous, and then you will have good success.

V. 9: Have I not commanded you? Be strong and of good courage; do not be afraid, nor be dismayed, for the Lord your God is with you wherever you go."

V. 10: Then Joshua commanded the officers of the people, saying,

V. 11: "Pass through the camp and command the people, saying, 'prepare provisions for yourselves, for within three days you will cross over the Jordan, to go in to possess the land which the Lord your God is giving you to possess.'"

V. 12: And to the Reubenites, the Gadites, and half the tribe of Manasseh Joshua spoke, saying,

V. 13: Remember the word which Moses the servant of the Lord commanded you, saying, 'The Lord your God is giving you rest and is giving you this land.'

V. 14: Your wives, your little ones, and your livestock shall remain in the land which Moses gave you on this side of the Jordan. But you shall pass before your brethren armed, all your mighty men of valor, and help them,

V. 15: until the Lord has given your brethren rest, as He gave you, and they also have taken possession of the land which the Lord your God is given them. Then you shall return to the land of your possession and enjoy it, which Moses the Lord's servant gave you on t-his side of the Jordan towards the sunrise."

V. 16: So they answered Joshua, saying, all that you command us we will do, and wherever you send us we will go.

V. 17: Just as we heeded Moses in all things, we will heed you. Only the Lord your God be with you, as He was with Moses.

V. 18: Whoever rebels against your command and does not heed your words, in all that you command him, shall be put to death. Only be strong and of good courage.

Exodus 28:1: Now take Aaron your brother, and his sons with him, from among the children of Israel, that he may

	minister to Me as priest, Aaron and Aaron's sons: Nadab, Abihu, Eleazar, and Ithamar.
Judges 2:16:	Nevertheless, the Lord raised up judges who delivered them out of the hand of those who plundered them.
1 Samuel 10:1:	Then Samuel took a flask of oil and poured it on his head, and kissed him and said: "Is it not because the Lord has anointed you commander over His inheritance?
1 Samuel 13:14:	But now your kingdom shall not continue. The Lord has sought for Himself a man after His own heart, and the Lord has commanded him to be commander over His people, because you have not kept what the Lord commanded you."

2 Samuel 7
- V. 1: Now it came to pass when the king was dwelling in his house, and the Lord had given him rest from all his enemies all around,
- V. 2: that the king said to Nathan the prophet, "See now, I dwell in a house of cedar, but the Ark of God dwells inside tent curtains."
- V. 3: Then Nathan said to the king, "Go do all that is in your heart, for the Lord is with you."
- V. 4: But it happened that night that the word of the Lord came to Nathan, saying,
- V. 5: "Go and tell My servant David, Thus says the Lord: Would you build a house for me to dwell in?
- V. 6: For I have not dwelt in a house since the time that I brought the children of Israel up from Egypt, even to this day, but have moved about in a tent and in a tabernacle.
- V. 7: Wherever I have moved about with the children of Israel, have I ever spoken a word to anyone from the tribes of Israel, whom I commanded to shepherd My people Israel, saying, "Why have you not built Me a house of cedar?"
- V. 8: Now therefore, thus shall you say to My servant David, "Thus says the Lord of hosts: "I took you from the sheepfold, from following the sheep, to be ruler over My people, over Israel.
- V. 9: And I have been with you wherever you have gone, and have cut off all your enemies from before you, and have made you a great name,

like the name of the great men who are on the earth.

V. 10: Moreover I will appoint a place for My people Israel, and will plant them, that they may dwell in a place of their own and move no more; nor shall the sons of wickedness oppress them anymore, as previously.

V. 11: since the time that I commanded judges to be over My people Israel, and have caused you rest from all your enemies. Also the Lord tells you that He will make you a house.

V. 12: when you days are fulfilled and you rest with your fathers, I will set up your seed after you, who will come from your body, and I will establish his kingdom.

V. 13: He shall build a house for My name, and I will establish the throne of his kingdom forever.

V. 14: I will be his father, and he shall be My son. If he commits iniquity, I will chasten him with the rod of men and with the blows of the sons of men.

V. 15: But My mercy shall not depart from him, as I took it from Saul, whom I removed from before you.

V. 16: And your house and your kingdom shall be established forever before you. Your throne shall be established forever."

V. 17: According to all these words and according to all this vision, so Nathan spoke to David.

V. 18: Then King David went in and sat before the Lord, and said, Who am I, 0 Lord God? And what is my house, that you have brought me this far?

V. 19: And this was a small thing in your sight, 0 Lord God; and you have also spoken of your servant's house for a great while to come. Is this the manner of man, O Lord God?

2 Samuel 7

V. 20: Now what more can David say to you? For you, Lord God, know your servant.

V. 21: For your word's sake, and according to your own heart, You have done all these great things to make Your servant know them.

V. 22: Therefore You are great, 0 Lord God. For there is none like You, nor is there any God beside You, according to all that we have heard with our ears.

V. 23: And who is like Your people, like Israel, the one nation on earth whom God went to redeem as His people to make for Himself a name-and to do for Yourself great and awesome deeds for Your land-before Your people whom You redeemed for Yourself from Egypt, the nations, and their Gods?

V. 24: For You have made Your people Israel Your very own people forever; and You, Lord, have become their God.

V. 25: Now, O Lord God, the word which You have spoken concerning your servant and concerning his house, establish it forever and do as You have said.

V. 26: So let your name be magnified forever, saying, "The Lord of hosts is the God over Israel." And let the house of Your servant David be established before you.

V. 27: For you, O Lord of hosts, God of Israel, have revealed this to Your servant, saying, 'I will build you a house.' Therefore Your servant has found it in his heart to pray this prayer to You.

V. 28: And now, O Lord God, You are God, and Your words are true, and You have promised this goodness to Your servant.

V. 29: Now therefore, let it please You to bless the house of Your servant, that it may continue before You forever; for You, O Lord God, have spoken it, and with Your blessing let the house of Your servant be blessed forever.

1 Corinthians 12:28: And God has appointed these in the church: first Apostles, second prophets, third teachers, after that miracles, then gifts of healings, helps, administration, varieties of tongues.

Psalm 75:6-7

V. 6: for exaltation comes neither from the east nor from the west nor from the south.

V. 7: But God is the judge: He puts down one and exalts another.

Luke 22:26: But not so among you; on the contrary, he who is greatest among you, let him be as the younger, and he who governs as he who serves.

Deuteronomy 17:20: That his heart may not be lifted above his brethren, that he may not turn aside from the commandment to the right nor to the left, and that he may prolong his days in his kingdom, he and his children in the midst of Israel.

1 Corinthians 15:9-10
V. 9:   For I am the least of the apostles, who am not worthy to be called an Apostle, because I persecuted the church of God.
V. 10: But by the Grace of God I am what I am, and His Grace toward me was not in vain; but I labored more abundantly than they all, yet not I, but the Grace of God which was with me.

Hebrews 13:17:   Obey those who rule over you, and be submissive, for they watch out for your souls, as those who must give account. Let them do so with joy and not with grief, for that would be unprofitable for you.

1 Peter 5:2-3
V. 2:   Shepherd the flock of God which is among you, serving as overseers, not by compulsion but willingly, not for dishonest gain but eagerly;
V. 3:   nor as being lords over those entrusted to you, but being examples to the flock.

1 Peter 4:10:   As each one has received a gift, minister it to one another, as good stewards of the manifold Grace of God.

Numbers 16:9-33
V. 9:   Is it a small thing to you that the God of Israel has separated you from the congregation of Israel, to bring you near to Himself, to do the work of the tabernacle of the Lord, and to stand before the congregation to serve them;
V. 10: and that He has brought you near to Himself, you and all your brethren, the sons of Levi with you? And are you seeking the priesthood also?
V. 11: Therefore you and all your company are gathered together against the Lord. And what is Aaron that you complain against him?
V. 12: And Moses sent to call Dathan and Abiram the sons of Eliab, but they said, "We will not come up!

Numbers 16
V. 13: Is it a small thing that you have brought us up out of a land flowing with milk and honey, to kill us in the wilderness, that you should keep acting like a prince over us?
V. 14: Moreover, you have not brought us into a land flowing with milk

and honey, nor given us inheritance of fields and vineyards. Will you put out the eyes of these men? We will not come up!"

V. 15: Then Moses was very angry, and said to the Lord, "Do not respect their offering. I have not taken one donkey from them, nor have I hurt one of them.

V. 16: And Moses said to Korah, "Tomorrow, you and all your company be present before the Lord-you and they, as well as Aaron.

V. 17: Let each take his censer and put incense in it, and each of you bring his censer before the Lord, two hundred and fifty censers; both you and Aaron, each with his censer."

V. 18: So every man took his censer, put fire in it, laid incense on it, and stood at the door of the tabernacle of meeting with Moses and Aaron.

V. 19: And Korah gathered all the congregation against them at the door of the tabernacle of meeting. Then the glory of the Lord appeared to all the congregation.

V. 20: And the Lord spoke to Moses and Aaron, saying,

V. 21: Separate yourselves from among this congregation, that I may consume them in a moment."

V. 22: Then they fell on their faces, and said, "O God, the God of the Spirits of all flesh, shall one man sin, and you be angry with all the congregation?

V. 23: So the Lord spoke to Moses, saying,

V. 24: "Speak to the congregation, saying, 'Get away from the tents of Korah, Dathan, and Abiram.'"

V. 25: Then Moses rose and went to Dathan and Abiram, and the elders of Israel followed him.

V. 26: And he spoke to the congregation, saying, Depart now from the tents of these wicked men! Touch nothing of theirs, lest you be consumed in all their sin.

V. 27: So they got away from around the tents of Korah, Dathan, and Abiram; and Dathan and Abiram came out and stood in the door of their tents, with their wives, their sons, and their little 0hildren.

V. 28: And Moses said: "By this you shall know that the Lord has sent me to do all these works, for I have not done them of my own will.

Numbers 16

V. 29: If these men die naturally like all men, or if they are visited by the common fate of men, then the Lord has not sent me.

V. 30: But if the Lord creates a new thing, and the earth opens its mouth and swallows them up and all that belongs to them. And they go down alive into the pit, then you will understand that these men have rejected the Lord.

V. 31: Now it came to pass, as he had finished speaking all these words, that the ground split apart under them,

V. 32: and the earth opened its mouth and swallowed them up, and all the men with Korah, with their goods.

V. 33: So they and all those with them went down alive into the pit; the earth closed over them, and they perished from among the assembly.

Mark 10:35-45

V. 35: Then James and John, the sons of Zebedee, came to Him, saying, "Teacher, we want You to do for us whatever we ask.

V. 36: And He said to them, "What do you want Me to do for you?

V. 37: They said to Him, "Grant us that we may sit, one on Your right hand and the other on Your left, in your glory.

V. 38: But Jesus said to them, "You do not know what you ask. Are you able to drink the cup that I drink, and be baptized with the baptism I am baptized with?"

V. 39: They said to Him, "We are able." So Jesus said to them, "You will indeed drink the cup that I drink, and with the baptism I am baptized with you will be baptized;

V. 40: but to sit on My right hand and on My left is not mine to give, but is for chose for whom it is prepared."

V. 41: And when the ten heard it, they began to be greatly displeased with James and John.

V. 42: But Jesus called them to Himself and said to them, "You know that those who are considered rulers over the Gentiles lord it over them, and their great ones exercise authority over them.

V. 43: Yet it shall not be so among you; but whoever desires to become great among you shall be your servant.

V. 44: And whoever of you desires to be first shall be slave to all.

V. 45: For even the son of man did not come to be served, but to serve, and give His life a ransom for many."

Leaders are Accountable

Hebrews 13: 17: Obey those who rule over you, and be submissive, for they watch out for your souls as those who must give account. Let them do so with joy and not with grief, for that would be unprofitable for you.

Luke 12:48: But he who did not know, yet committed things deserving of stripes, shall be beaten with few. For everyone to whom much is given, from him much will be required; and to whom much has been committed, of him they will ask the more.

Numbers 20: 12: Then the Lord spoke to Moses and Aaron, "Because you did not believe Me, to hallow Me in the eyes of the children of Israel, therefore you shall not bring this assembly in the land which I have given them."

James 3: 1: My brethren let not many of you become teachers, knowing that we shall receive a stricter judgment.

Faith and Leadership

Philippians 2: 13: for it is God who works in you to will and to do for His good pleasure.

1 Corinthians 15:10: But by the Grace of God I am what I am, and His Grace toward me was not in vain; but I labored more abundantly than you all, yet not I, but the Grace of God which was with me.

1 Samuel 2:3: Talk no more so very proudly; Let no arrogance come from your mouth, for the Lord is the God of knowledge; and by Him actions are weighed.

2 Timothy 4:7: I have fought the good fight, I have finished the race, I have kept the faith.

Exodus 18:25: And Moses chose able men out of Israel, and made them heads over the people: rulers of thousands, rulers of hundreds, rulers of fifties, and rulers of tens.

Isaiah 53:6: All we like sheep have gone astray; we have turned everyone to his own way; And the Lord has laid on

Him the iniquity of us all.

Exodus 18:13-27

V. 13: And so it was, on the next day, that Moses sat to judge the people, and the people stood before Moses from morning until evening.

V. 14: So when Moses' father-in-law saw all that he did for the people, he said, "What is this thing that you are doing for the people? Why do you alone sit, and all the people stand before from morning until evening?"

V. 15: And Moses said to his father-in-law, "Because the people come to me to inquire of God.

V. 16: When they have a difficulty they come to me, and I judge between one and another; and I make known the statutes of God and His laws.

V. 17: So Moses' father-in-law said to him, "The thing that you do is not good."

V. 18: Both you and these people who are with you will surely wear yourselves out. For this thing is too much for you: You are not able to perform it by yourself.

V. 19: Listen now to my voice; I will give you counsel, and God will be with you: Stand before God for the people, so that you may bring the difficulties to God.

V. 20: And you shall teach them the statutes of the laws, and show them the way in which they must walk and the work they must do.

V. 21: Moreover you shall select from all the people able men, such as fear God, men of truth, hating covetousness; and place such over them to be rulers over thousands, rulers over hundreds, rulers over fifties, and rulers over tens.

V. 22: and let them judge the people at all times. Then it will be that every great matter they shall bring to you, but every small matter they themselves shall judge. So it will be easier for you, for they will hear the burden with you.

V. 23: If you do this thing, and God so commands you, then you will be able to endure, and all the people will go to their place in peace."

V. 24: So Moses heeded the voice of his father-in-law and did all that he had said.

V. 25: And Moses chose able men out of Israel, and made them heads over the people: rulers over thousands, rulers over hundreds, rulers over fifties, rulers over tens.

V. 26: So they judged the people at all times; the hard cases they brought to Moses, but they judged every small case themselves.

V. 27: Then Moses let his father-in-law depart, and he went his own way to his own land.

1 Chronicles 24

V. 1: Now there are the divisions of the sons of Aaron. The sons of Aaron were Nadab, Abihu, Eleazar, and Ithamar.

V. 2: And Nadab and Abihu died before their father; and had no children; therefore Eleazar and Ithamar ministered as priests.

V. 3: Then David with Zadok of the sons of Eleazar, and Ahimelech the sons of Ithamar, divided them according to the schedule of their service.

V. 4: There were more leaders found of the sons of Eleazar than of the sons of Ithamar, and thus they were divided. Among the sons of Eleazar were sixteen heads of their fathers' houses, and eight heads of their fathers' houses among the sons of Ithamar.

V. 5: Thus they were divided by lot, one group as another, for there were officials of the sanctuary and officials of the house of God, from the sons of Eleazar and from the sons of Ithamar.

V. 6: And the scribe, Shemaiah the son of Nethanel, one of the Levites, wrote them down before the king, the leaders, Zadok, the priest, Ahimelech the son of Abiathar, and the heads of the fathers' houses of the priests and Levites, one father's house taken for Eleazar and one taken for Ithamar.

V. 7: Now the first lot fell to Jehoiarib, the second to Jedaiah,

V. 8: the third to Harim, the fourth to Seorim,

V. 9: the fifth to Malchijah, the sixth to Mijamin,

V. 10: the seventh to Hakkoz, the eighth to Abijah, V 11: the ninth to Jeshua, the tenth to Shecaniah,

V. 12: the eleventh to Eliashib, the twelfth to Jakim,

V. 13: the thirteenth to Huppah, the fourteenth to Jeshebeab, V 14: the fifteenth to Bilgah, the sixteenth to Immer

V. 15: the seventeenth to Hezir, the eighteenth to Happizzez V 16: the nineteenth to Pethahiah, the twentieth to Jehezekel,

V. 17: the twenty-first to Jachin, the twenty-second to Gamul

V. 18: the twenty-third to Delaiah, the twenty-fourth to Maaziah.

V. 19: This was their schedule for coming into the house of the Lord according to their ordinances by the hand of Aaron their father, as the Lord God of Israel had commanded him.

V. 20: And the rest of the sons of Levi: of the sons of Amram, "Shubeal; of

the sons of Shubael, Jehdeiaah.
V. 21: Concerning Rehabiah, the sons of Rahabiah, the first was Isshiah.
V. 22: Of the Izharites, Shelomoth; of the sons of Sheomoth, Jahath.
V. 23: Of the sons of Hebron, Jeriah was the first, Amariah the second, Jahaziel the third, and Jekameam the fourth.
V. 24: Of the sons of Uzziel, Michah; of the sons ofMichah, Shamir.
V. 25: the brother of Michah, Isshiah; of the sons of Isshiah, Zechariah.
V. 26: The sons of Merari were Mahli and Mushi; the sons of Jazziah, Beno,
V. 27: The sons of Merari by Jaaziah were Beno, Shoham, Zaccur, and Ibri.
V. 28: Of Mahli: Eleazar, who had no sons
V. 29: Of Kish: the son of Kish, Jerahmeel.
V. 30: Also the sons of Mushi were Mahli, Eder, and Jerimoth. These were the sons of the Levites according to their father's houses.
V. 31: These also cast lots just as their brothers the sons of Aaron did, in the presence of King David, Zadok, Ahimelech, and the heads of the fathers' houses of the priests and Levites. The chief fathers did just as their younger brothers.

1 Timothy 3:4-5
V. 4: One who rules his own house well, having his children in submission with all reverence
V. 5: (for if a man does not know how to rule his own house, how will he take care of the church of God?)

Romans 13:1: Let every soul be subject to the governing authorities. For there is no authority except from God, and the authorities that exist are appointed by God.

Luke 7:6-9
V. 6: Then Jesus went with them. And when He was ready not far from the house, the centurion sent friends to Him, saying to Him, "Lord, do not trouble yourself, for I am not worthy that You should enter under my roof.
V. 7: Therefore I did not even think myself worthy to come to You. But say the word and my servant will be healed.
V. 8: For I am also a man placed under authority, having soldiers under me. And I say to one, "Go and he goes; and I say to another, 'Come,' and he comes: and to my servant, 'Do this,' and he does it."
V. 9: When Jesus heard these things, He marveled at him, and turned

around and said to the crowd that followed Him, "I say to you, I have not found such great faith, not even in Israel!"

Hebrews 11
- V. 24: (Faith) By faith Moses, when he became of age, refused to be called the son of Pharaoh's daughter,
- V. 25: (Integrity) choosing rather to suffer affliction with the people of God than to enjoy the passing pleasures of sin.
- V. 26: (Vision) esteeming the reproach of Christ greater riches than the treasures in Egypt; for he looked to be rewarded.
- V. 27: (Decisiveness) By faith he forsook Egypt, not fearing the wrath of the king; for he endured as seeing Him who is invisible
- V. 28: (Obedience) By faith he kept the Passover and the sprinkling of blood, lest he who destroyed the firstborn should touch them.
- V. 29: (Responsibility) By faith they passed by the Red Sea as by dry land, whereas the Egyptians, attempting to do so were drowned.

Benjamin A. Van Winkle

Christian Leadership

Benjamin A. Van Winkle

www.ingramcontent.com/pod-product-compliance
Lightning Source LLC
Chambersburg PA
CBHW021157080526
44588CB00008B/378